Urban Beekeeping: Managing Hives in City Environments

By Anthony Carter

Stay connected and further your journey into urban beekeeping by signing up for my newsletter!

Visit this page of my blog **www.beekeeping-101.com/newsletter** to subscribe and receive the latest tips, stories, and updates right to your inbox.

If you enjoy this journey through "Urban Beekeeping: Managing Hives in City Environments," I would be very grateful if you could take a moment to leave a review on the platform from which you purchased this book. Your feedback not only supports me, but it also helps other aspiring urban beekeepers find their way. Thank you for being a part of my community and for contributing to the sustainable future of urban beekeeping.

Disclaimer

This book, "Urban Beekeeping: Managing Hives in City Environments," is provided for general informational purposes only. The author and publisher have made every effort to ensure the accuracy and reliability of the information provided within these pages. However, the information is provided "as is" without warranty of any kind.

The author and publisher do not guarantee or warrant that the techniques and strategies discussed in this book will be suitable for every individual or situation or that they are in compliance with local, state, or national laws. The author and publisher shall not be held liable for any direct, indirect, incidental, or consequential damages or any damages whatsoever arising from the use or performance of this book.

Urban beekeeping laws and regulations vary significantly by location. It is the reader's responsibility to ensure that their beekeeping practices are in compliance with the current laws and regulations of their area. The author and publisher advise readers to consult with local beekeeping associations, agricultural extension services, or governmental bodies for the most current information regarding urban beekeeping laws and best practices.

This book does not provide medical or legal advice. The information on bee stings, allergic reactions, or any other health-related topics should be considered as general information only and not a substitute for professional medical advice. Always seek the advice of a qualified healthcare provider with any questions you may have regarding a medical condition.

By reading this book, you agree that the author and publisher are not responsible for your success or failure resulting from the application of any information presented within these pages.

Table of Contents

Preface

Welcome to "Urban Beekeeping: Managing Hives in City Environments," a comprehensive guide designed to navigate the unique challenges and opportunities of keeping bees in urban settings. This book is crafted for city dwellers who dream of bringing a piece of the countryside into their urban existence, contributing to biodiversity, and embarking on a rewarding journey of beekeeping right in their backyards, rooftops, or balconies.

Urban environments offer a unique setting for beekeeping. Amidst the concrete jungle, bees play a crucial role in pollinating urban gardens, parks, and green spaces, helping to maintain the health and diversity of plant life. Their presence in cities supports local food production and brings awareness to the importance of pollinators in our ecosystems. However, managing hives in densely populated areas comes with its own set of challenges—from navigating local regulations to ensuring the safety and acceptance of bees in community spaces.

This book is born out of a necessity to bridge the gap between traditional beekeeping practices and the modern urban landscape. It aims to equip you with the knowledge, skills, and confidence to successfully manage bee hives in city environments. Whether you are a beginner with a budding interest in beekeeping or an experienced beekeeper looking to adapt your practices to an urban setting, this guide offers something for everyone.

We will explore the essentials of urban beekeeping, including selecting the right bee species for city life, understanding and complying with local laws, and engaging positively with neighbors and the community. Practical advice on setting up and managing your hives in limited spaces, maintaining the health of your colonies, and harvesting honey, will provide you with a solid foundation to thrive in urban beekeeping. Moreover, this book delves into the ethical considerations and responsibilities that come with keeping bees in urban areas, emphasizing the importance of sustainable practices and community engagement.

"Urban Beekeeping: Managing Hives in City Environments" also addresses the challenges unique to urban settings, offering solutions and innovative approaches to overcome them. From dealing with pests and diseases to ensuring your bees have access to adequate forage, each chapter is filled with detailed information, practical tips, and insights to guide you through your urban beekeeping journey.

As cities continue to grow and green spaces become ever more precious, the role of urban beekeepers has never been more critical. By fostering healthy bee populations, we contribute to the well-being of our urban ecosystems, enhance biodiversity, and bring the community closer to nature. This book is a testament to the resilience and adaptability of bees and their keepers, highlighting the beauty and challenges of keeping bees in the heart of the city.

Join us on this exciting journey into the world of urban beekeeping, where every hive contributes to a greener, more sustainable urban future.

Chapter 1: Understanding Urban Beekeeping

Urban beekeeping is an emerging trend that brings the ancient practice of beekeeping into the heart of our cities, offering a unique blend of challenges and opportunities for enthusiasts and environmentalists alike. This chapter serves as your gateway to the world of urban beekeeping, laying the groundwork for a deeper understanding of how beekeeping can thrive within the urban jungle. Here, we embark on a journey to explore the fundamentals of urban beekeeping, shining a light on the pivotal role bees play in enhancing urban ecosystems, supporting biodiversity, and contributing to local food sustainability.

In today's rapidly urbanizing world, the importance of bees goes beyond rural fields and into the concrete landscapes of our cities. Urban beekeeping not only offers a fascinating hobby for city dwellers but also presents a critical opportunity to contribute positively to our urban environments. This chapter aims to equip you with the foundational knowledge required to navigate the exciting and sometimes complex world of keeping bees in urban settings. From understanding the ecological impact of urban bees to tackling the common myths that surround urban beekeeping, we delve into the essential aspects that every aspiring urban beekeeper should know.

The role of bees in pollinating urban gardens, parks, and balconies makes them invaluable allies in maintaining and enhancing urban biodiversity. Their presence in cities supports not just the local flora, but also promotes a wider environmental awareness and connection to nature among urban communities. However, the practice of urban beekeeping comes with its unique set of challenges, from navigating space constraints to ensuring a harmonious coexistence with neighbors and local wildlife. Moreover, the myths surrounding beekeeping in urban environments often deter many potential beekeepers from starting their journey.

In this chapter, we aim to dispel these myths and provide a clear, evidence-based insight into the realities of urban beekeeping. We'll explore the benefits it brings to urban environments, the challenges faced by urban beekeepers, and the truth behind common misconceptions. By understanding the significance of bees in urban ecosystems, the practicalities of keeping bees in cities, and the positive impact urban beekeeping can have, readers will be well-prepared to take the next steps in their urban beekeeping adventure.

Embark with us on this enlightening journey through the heart of urban beekeeping, where we will lay the foundation for a rewarding partnership between humans and bees in the urban landscape. Whether you are a seasoned beekeeper looking to adapt your practice to an urban setting or a newcomer curious about the role of bees in city life, this chapter will provide you with the insights and inspiration needed to appreciate and contribute to the fascinating world of urban beekeeping.

The Role of Bees in the Urban Ecosystem

Pollination and Biodiversity

In the bustling environment of our cities, where concrete often overshadows green, the role of bees becomes more crucial than ever. Urban beekeeping emerges not just as a hobby or passion, but as a vital contributor to the ecological health and biodiversity of our urban landscapes. Bees, nature's master pollinators, embark daily on their critical mission, transferring pollen from one flower to another, ensuring the continuation of many plant species. This seemingly simple act of pollination is the cornerstone of the reproductive processes for a vast majority of flowering plants, playing a pivotal role in the production of fruits, vegetables, and seeds that constitute a significant portion of the food sources for a variety of urban wildlife and humans alike.

In urban settings, the presence of bees takes on an added layer of importance. Green spaces, such as parks, gardens, and even rooftop greeneries, are often isolated islands in a sea of asphalt and buildings. Bees help bridge these gaps, ensuring cross-pollination occurs across these fragmented landscapes. This not only aids in the health and spread of these plant species but also in increasing their genetic diversity, which is crucial for resilience against diseases, pests, and changing climate conditions.

Moreover, bees' role in urban ecosystems extends beyond just the pollination of commercial crops and garden plants. They also pollinate wild flora, contributing to the health and spread of native plant species, which in turn supports a wide range of urban wildlife. Birds, small mammals, and other insects rely on these plants for food and habitat, creating a complex web of urban biodiversity that enriches our cities in unseen ways.

The introduction of beekeeping into urban areas has the potential to significantly enhance local biodiversity. Bees in cities can thrive, given the right conditions, often benefiting from a wider variety of plant species and longer blooming periods because of the urban heat island effect, which keeps cities warmer than their rural counterparts. This not only extends the foraging season for bees, but also ensures a more diverse and continuous supply of pollen and nectar.

Urban beekeeping, therefore, stands as a testament to the symbiotic relationship between humans and nature. It highlights how urban spaces can be transformed into thriving ecosystems that support both biodiversity and the well-being of the community. By fostering healthy bee populations, cities can become more resilient, vibrant, and life-sustaining environments. The act of keeping bees in urban areas not only contributes to the global effort to protect these indispensable pollinators but also reconnects urban dwellers with the natural world, reminding us of the critical role we all play in preserving our planet's biodiversity.

Benefits to Urban Gardens and Green Spaces

The presence of bees in urban areas extends far beyond the realm of pollination, significantly enhancing the vitality and productivity of urban gardens and community green spaces. These tiny pollinators play a pivotal role in transforming city landscapes into lush, green havens that yield an abundance of fruits, vegetables, and flowers. The interaction between bees and these green spaces creates a cycle of growth and sustainability that enriches urban environments in multiple ways.

Enhancing Productivity of Urban Gardens

One of the most immediate benefits of urban beekeeping is the noticeable increase in the productivity of urban gardens. Bees, by their very nature, are efficient and tireless pollinators, visiting thousands of flowers each day. This relentless pursuit of nectar and pollen results in the effective pollination of a wide array of plant species. For urban gardeners, this translates to higher yields of fruits and vegetables, ensuring that garden spaces are not only visually appealing but also productive food sources. The diversity of crops that bees pollinate is extensive, ranging from common vegetables and fruits to the flowering plants that add beauty and color to the urban landscape.

Encouraging Plant Diversity

Beyond increasing yields, bees also encourage the growth of a wider variety of plants. Their pollination activities help ensure the propagation of plants, leading to a more diverse and resilient green space. This diversity is crucial for the health of urban gardens and parks, as it creates a more stable ecosystem that can better resist pests and diseases. Moreover, a diverse plant life attracts a variety of wildlife, contributing to the ecological balance within urban areas. Birds, butterflies, and beneficial insects are drawn to these spaces, creating a vibrant and dynamic urban ecosystem.

Creating Essential Habitats for Wildlife

Urban gardens and green spaces serve as critical habitats for wildlife, offering refuge and resources in the midst of urban sprawl. By enhancing the productivity and diversity of these areas, bees play a vital role in maintaining these urban oases. These habitats are essential for the survival of many species, providing food, shelter, and breeding grounds. The presence of bees and the pollination services they provide help ensure that these green spaces remain thriving ecosystems capable of supporting a wide range of urban wildlife.

Improving the Overall Quality of Life in Cities

The benefits of urban beekeeping extend to the overall quality of life for city dwellers. Green spaces enhanced by bee activity offer recreational and aesthetic value, contributing to the mental and physical well-being of the urban population. Gardens and parks become more inviting and enjoyable, serving as peaceful retreats from the hustle and bustle of city life. Furthermore, the increased productivity of urban gardens can lead to more local and sustainable food sources, contributing to the health and nutrition of the community.

In essence, urban beekeepers play a critical role in fostering vibrant and productive green spaces within cities. The relationship between bees and these areas exemplifies the interconnectedness of all living things and highlights the positive impact that urban beekeeping can have on the environment and the community. By supporting bee populations in urban areas, we not only enhance the biodiversity and productivity of our gardens and parks, but also contribute to the creation of healthier, more sustainable urban environments.

Urban Beekeeping: Myths vs. Reality

Dispelling Common Myths

Urban beekeeping, while growing in popularity, is still shrouded in a cloud of myths and misconceptions that can intimidate or mislead potential beekeepers. These myths not only obscure the truth about urban beekeeping but also hinder the growth of urban bee populations and their positive impact on city environments. Here, we aim to confront these myths head-on, dispelling them with facts and evidence to encourage more city dwellers to embark on the rewarding journey of beekeeping.

Myth 1: Bees are More Aggressive in Urban Areas

One of the most pervasive myths is that bees become more aggressive in urban settings. This misconception likely stems from a misunderstanding of bee behavior and the assumption that urban noise and activity stress bees, leading to increased aggression. However, research and practical experience show that bees' temperament is more closely related to their species and hive conditions than to their urban or rural location. Many urban beekeepers report that their bees are docile and that with proper handling and hive management, instances of aggression are minimal. Urban environments can actually offer a calmer setting for bees because of the reduced use of agricultural pesticides and the availability of diverse plant sources.

Myth 2: Cities are Unsuitable for Beekeeping Because of Pollution

Concerns about air pollution and its effects on bees can deter urban residents from considering beekeeping. While it's true that cities can have higher levels of pollution, bees have shown remarkable resilience and adaptability. Studies have indicated that bees can thrive in urban environments, often outperforming their rural counterparts in health and honey production. The variety of flowering plants in gardens, parks, and balconies throughout the city can provide bees with a diverse and continuous food source, mitigating the potential negative affects of urban pollution.

Myth 3: Lack of Green Spaces Makes Cities Inhospitable to Bees

Another common myth is that the concrete landscapes of cities offer little to no green space for bees to forage, making urban areas inhospitable for beekeeping. In reality, urban gardens, parks, and rooftop green spaces can create rich environments for bees, often with a greater variety of plants than found in monoculture rural areas. Urban beekeepers play a crucial role in supplementing these green spaces by planting bee-friendly flora, ensuring that bees have ample forage. Cities can become biodiversity hotspots, supporting healthy bee populations that, in turn, contribute to the urban ecosystem's vitality.

Conclusion

Dispelling these myths is essential for the growth and acceptance of urban beekeeping. Understanding the realities of keeping bees in urban environments opens the door for more individuals to contribute positively to their local ecosystems through beekeeping. By providing evidence-based information and challenging misconceptions, we can encourage a more informed and enthusiastic community of urban beekeepers. The truth is that urban environments offer unique opportunities for beekeeping, with potential benefits that far outweigh the challenges. With the right knowledge and resources, urban beekeeping can flourish, supporting both the bees and the broader urban ecosystem.

Real Benefits and Challenges of Urban Beekeeping

The practice of urban beekeeping, while shrouded in various myths and misconceptions, holds tangible benefits for the urban ecosystem, bee populations, and beekeepers alike. However, it's essential to approach this practice with a clear understanding of both its advantages and the challenges it presents. This balanced perspective ensures that urban beekeepers are well-prepared to navigate the complexities of beekeeping in urban settings and contribute positively to their communities and the environment.

Enhancing Local Biodiversity

One of the most significant benefits of urban beekeeping is its contribution to local biodiversity. By providing bees with habitats in urban areas, beekeepers help maintain and increase the diversity of plant and animal life. Bees act as crucial pollinators for city gardens, parks, and wild areas, supporting the growth of a wide array of plant species. This, in turn, supports a variety of urban wildlife, creating a richer, more resilient urban ecosystem.

Supporting Community Green Initiatives

Urban beekeeping often goes hand in hand with community green initiatives, such as the creation of pollinator gardens, green roofs, and sustainability projects. Beekeepers can become active participants in local environmental efforts, promoting awareness and action towards creating greener, more sustainable urban spaces. The presence of bees can serve as a catalyst for community engagement, encouraging people to consider their impact on the local ecosystem and take steps towards enhancing it.

Producing Local Honey

Another tangible benefit of urban beekeeping is the production of local honey. Urban honey is not only a sustainable food source, but also a unique product that reflects the local flora. It can help raise awareness about the importance of bees and pollination, and its sale can support local economies and beekeeping initiatives. Moreover, urban honey often has distinct flavors, making it a favorite among local food enthusiasts and promoting a connection between urban dwellers and their natural environment.

Navigating Local Regulations

One of the primary challenges faced by urban beekeepers is navigating the maze of local regulations related to beekeeping. Many cities have specific ordinances that govern the practice, including restrictions on the number of hives, hive placements, and the requirement for permits or notifications. Prospective beekeepers must familiarize themselves with these regulations to ensure their beekeeping activities are legal and compliant, avoiding potential conflicts and fostering positive relationships with their communities.

Managing Space Constraints

Space constraints are another significant challenge in urban beekeeping. Unlike rural environments, where beekeepers often have ample space for their hives, urban beekeepers must make do with limited areas such as

©Anthony Carter | www.beekeeping-101.com |part of Carman Online Content Publishing Ltd

rooftops, balconies, or small backyards. This requires creative solutions and careful planning to ensure the bees have enough space to thrive without causing issues for neighbors or the beekeepers themselves.

Ensuring Health and Safety

The health and safety of both bees and the public are paramount in urban beekeeping. Beekeepers must take steps to manage their hives responsibly, ensuring bees are healthy, not overly aggressive, and that their foraging does not become a nuisance to people, especially those with allergies. Public education and engagement are crucial in this regard, as they can help mitigate fears and misconceptions about bees, promoting coexistence and appreciation for these essential pollinators.

Urban beekeeping presents a unique blend of opportunities and challenges that require careful consideration and responsible management. By understanding the real benefits and addressing the challenges head-on, urban beekeepers can make a positive impact on their local environments, contributing to the sustainability and resilience of urban ecosystems.

Pollination in Urban Settings

The Importance of Urban Forage

In the concrete landscapes of urban settings, the quest for sufficient forage emerges as a significant challenge for bees and beekeepers alike. The dense urban fabric, characterized by its high-rise buildings and paved surfaces, often lacks the continuous stretches of natural habitats found in rural areas. This fragmentation of green spaces creates a unique hurdle for pollinators, necessitating a focused effort to identify and create viable forage opportunities within the city. Understanding the critical importance of urban forage is the first step toward sustaining healthy bee populations and, by extension, robust urban ecosystems.

Identifying Forage Opportunities

The foundation of supporting urban bees lies in recognizing the potential forage sources that cities can offer. Despite the apparent dominance of concrete, many urban areas are home to parks, roadside greenery, gardens, and even abandoned lots that can serve as vital forage sites for bees. Identifying these areas requires a collaborative effort among beekeepers, city planners, and the community to map out green spaces and assess their forage potential. By cataloging the types of flowering plants available and their blooming periods, urban beekeepers can strategize on how best to position their hives for optimal foraging success.

Planting Pollinator-Friendly Gardens

One of the most direct methods to enhance urban forage is through the establishment of pollinator-friendly gardens. This initiative can take place at various scales, from individual homeowners planting bee-friendly flowers in their yards to larger community efforts in public parks and green spaces. Selecting a diversity of plants that bloom at different times of the year is key to providing a consistent food source for bees. Encouraging the planting of native species can also have a dual benefit, supporting both the local bee populations and the overall biodiversity of the area.

Working with Local Parks and Green Spaces

Collaboration with local authorities to integrate pollinator-friendly practices in public parks and green spaces can significantly amplify the impact of urban beekeeping. This involves advocating for the inclusion of diverse, nectar-rich plants in landscaping projects and the reduction of pesticide use in these areas. Parks and community gardens can become sanctuaries for urban bees, offering ample foraging opportunities while simultaneously enhancing the aesthetic and recreational value of these spaces for the human population.

Encouraging Community Initiatives

The success of creating a flourishing urban forage landscape relies heavily on community involvement. Encouraging community initiatives to support urban bee populations can take many forms, from educational programs that raise awareness about the importance of pollinators to community planting days focused on enhancing green spaces with bee-friendly vegetation. Schools, businesses, and neighborhood associations can all play a role in fostering environments conducive to bee foraging, contributing to a collective effort that benefits both bees and the broader urban ecosystem.

The importance of urban forage cannot be overstated in the context of urban beekeeping. By identifying and creating forage opportunities, urban beekeepers and the community at large can ensure that bees thrive in city environments. This concerted effort not only supports the health and productivity of bee populations but also contributes to the resilience and vibrancy of urban ecosystems, making cities more livable for all their inhabitants.

Creating a Bee-Friendly Urban Environment

In the concrete landscapes of our cities, creating a bee-friendly environment presents a unique set of challenges and opportunities. Urban beekeepers stand at the forefront of this endeavor, playing a pivotal role in transforming urban areas into thriving habitats for bees. Their efforts not only support the needs of bee populations, but also contribute to the broader goal of promoting urban biodiversity and sustainability.

Advocating for Pollinator-Friendly Policies

One of the key ways urban beekeepers can make a difference is by advocating for pollinator-friendly policies at the local government level. This can include pushing for the planting of native, bee-attractive plants in public spaces such as parks, road medians, and community gardens. Beekeepers can also lobby for policies that limit the use of pesticides harmful to bees and encourage practices that support pollinator health. By working with city planners and policymakers, beekeepers help create an urban landscape that acknowledges and supports the crucial role of pollinators.

Engaging in Community Education

Education is a powerful tool in changing perceptions and fostering a bee-friendly urban environment. Urban beekeepers can engage with the community through workshops, school programs, and public demonstrations to raise awareness about the importance of bees in urban ecosystems. By demystifying bees and highlighting their benefits, beekeepers can alleviate fears and misconceptions, encouraging residents to welcome bees into their gardens and balconies. Educational initiatives can also inspire individuals and communities to take actionable steps towards creating bee-friendly spaces, such as planting pollinator gardens or reducing pesticide use.

Creating Partnerships with Local Organizations

Collaboration is essential in the effort to support urban bees. Beekeepers can forge partnerships with local organizations, such as environmental groups, gardening clubs, and schools, to amplify their impact. Together, they can initiate projects like creating pollinator pathways—networks of green spaces filled with native, flowering plants that provide bees with essential forage across urban landscapes. These partnerships can also facilitate the sharing of resources, knowledge, and advocacy efforts, making the push for a bee-friendly city a collective endeavor.

Increasing the Availability of Forage

Ensuring that bees have access to a continuous and diverse supply of forage is crucial in urban settings. Urban beekeepers can lead by example, planting a variety of flowering plants on their properties and encouraging others to do the same. Initiatives like "Bee the Change," which involve distributing seeds for bee-friendly plants to local residents, can make a significant impact. Additionally, beekeepers can work with local authorities to ensure that public spaces are landscaped with pollinators in mind, incorporating plants that bloom at different times of the year to provide bees with a steady source of nectar and pollen.

By taking these proactive steps, urban beekeepers play an instrumental role in creating a more bee-friendly environment within the city. Their efforts not only enhance the well-being of bees, but also contribute to the overall health of urban ecosystems. A city that supports its pollinators is a city that supports its residents, offering a richer, more biodiverse, and sustainable environment for all who live there.

Conclusion

Embarking on the journey of urban beekeeping opens up a world of opportunities to positively impact our urban environments, contribute to biodiversity, and engage with nature in the heart of the city. This initial chapter has laid the groundwork, offering a comprehensive overview of the fundamentals of urban beekeeping. By exploring the ecological importance of bees, addressing common myths, and highlighting the essential role of pollination in urban settings, we have started to unravel the complexities and delights of managing bees in city environments.

Understanding urban beekeeping is more than just a preliminary step; it's a critical foundation that informs every aspect of bee management in urban landscapes. It prepares you, the reader, to engage more deeply with the practical, hands-on aspects of beekeeping, from selecting hive locations to understanding the nuances of urban bee health and forage. This knowledge empowers you to make informed decisions, advocate for pollinator-friendly urban policies, and contribute to creating bee-friendly spaces within your community.

As we move forward into the subsequent chapters, we will dive into the specifics of setting up your urban beekeeping operation, navigating local regulations, managing hives in limited spaces, and much more. Each chapter builds upon this foundation, providing detailed guidance, practical advice, and innovative solutions to the unique challenges faced by urban beekeepers.

Equipped with the insights from this chapter, you are now ready to explore the fascinating and rewarding world of urban beekeeping. Whether you aim to start a single hive on a rooftop garden or manage multiple hives in a community space, the journey ahead is one of discovery, learning, and significant contribution to the sustainability and vibrancy of our cities.

Chapter 2: Getting Started with Urban Beekeeping

Embarking on the journey of urban beekeeping is an exciting endeavor, one that promises not only the joy of bee stewardship but also the opportunity to contribute positively to the urban ecosystem. However, like any worthwhile venture, it begins with preparation and understanding. This chapter is designed to guide aspiring urban beekeepers through the foundational steps necessary for successfully launching their beekeeping operations within the bustling confines of a city.

The transition from interest to action in urban beekeeping involves several crucial stages, each requiring careful consideration and planning. Initially, assessing the suitability of your urban environment for beekeeping is paramount. This step is not just about finding space; it's about understanding the unique challenges and opportunities your specific urban setting presents. Factors such as local flora, potential forage sources, and even the orientation of your beekeeping space can significantly impact the health and productivity of your urban bee colonies.

Selecting the right bee species for your urban environment is the next critical decision. Not all bees are created equal when it comes to thriving in city settings. Some species are better suited to the variable conditions and limited foraging options available in urban areas. The choice of species can affect everything from hive temperament to foraging habits, influencing both your experience as a beekeeper and the success of your hives.

Finally, gathering the essential equipment and supplies marks the transition from planning to practice. Beekeeping requires specific tools and resources, each serving a purpose in the management and care of your bees. From protective gear to hive materials, understanding what you need—and what you don't—is key to starting your beekeeping journey on the right foot.

This chapter will delve into each of these initial steps in detail, providing you with the knowledge and tools to assess your urban environment, choose the most suitable bee species, and equip yourself for the fascinating world of urban beekeeping. By laying a solid foundation, you'll be well on your way to becoming a successful urban beekeeper, ready to navigate the unique challenges and reap the rewards of keeping bees in a city environment. Let's embark on this journey together, step by informed step, into the rewarding practice of urban beekeeping.

Assessing Your Urban Environment

Evaluating Space and Sunlight

The first step in establishing an urban beekeeping operation is to assess the suitability of your available space. Whether you have access to a rooftop, a balcony, or a small backyard, understanding how to evaluate and optimize these areas for beekeeping is essential. This section will guide you through the key considerations, focusing on the critical aspects of space and sunlight exposure, to ensure your urban beekeeping venture starts on solid ground.

Understanding the Importance of Space

Space is a premium in urban environments, and the location you choose for your hive will significantly impact its success and the health of your bee colony. Bees require enough room to fly in and out of their hive without obstruction, and the hive itself needs to be situated in a stable, secure location where it won't be disturbed by pets, wildlife, or human activity. When evaluating your space, consider the following:

- **Accessibility:** Ensure the site is easily accessible for regular inspections and maintenance, as well as safe for honey harvesting activities.

- **Security:** The hive should be secure from tipping over because of strong winds or accidental bumps, particularly in high-rise balcony settings.
- **Space for Expansion:** Consider the potential for hive expansion. Bees can outgrow their initial setup, requiring additional space for extra boxes or even new hives.

Maximizing Sunlight Exposure

Sunlight plays a crucial role in the health and productivity of a bee colony. Bees are more active and thrive in sunny conditions, which helps regulate the temperature inside the hive, crucial for brood rearing and honey production. However, too much direct sunlight, especially in hotter climates, can overheat the hive. Balancing sunlight exposure is therefore key:

- **Orientation:** Position the hive entrance facing southeast to catch the early morning sun, encouraging worker bees to start foraging earlier.
- **Shade Considerations:** Provide partial shade to protect the hive from the intense midday and afternoon sun, especially during the hottest months. This can be achieved through natural shade from trees or by installing a protective cover that still allows for air circulation.
- **Ventilation:** Ensure there's adequate ventilation around the hive, particularly if it's located in a spot that receives extended periods of direct sunlight.

When assessing your urban environment for beekeeping, taking the time to carefully evaluate the available space and sunlight exposure will set the foundation for a healthy, productive bee colony. This involves not only understanding the physical dimensions and characteristics of your space but also considering the broader environmental factors that will influence your bees' well-being. By thoughtfully selecting and preparing your beekeeping site, you'll create an environment where your bees can flourish, contributing to the ecosystem and community of your urban area.

Understanding Local Flora and Forage Availability

The foundation of a thriving urban beekeeping operation lies in ensuring your bees have ample access to forage. In the dense fabric of the city, where natural habitats are often fragmented, understanding and enhancing the local flora available for your bees is crucial. This section guides you through assessing the types of flowering plants in your area, understanding their bloom seasons, and strategies to supplement urban forage, ensuring a consistent and nutritious food source for your colonies.

Identifying Local Forage Sources

Begin by identifying potential forage sources within flying distance of your proposed hive location—usually within a 3 to 5-mile radius. Urban environments can offer a diverse array of foraging opportunities for bees, from residential gardens and parklands to green roofs and community gardens. Pay special attention to native plant species, as these are often more attractive to local bees and provide higher nutritional value. Municipal parks departments, local beekeeping associations, and botanical gardens can be valuable resources for information on local flora.

Mapping Bloom Seasons

Understanding the bloom seasons of local plants is essential for ensuring your bees have a continuous source of nectar and pollen. Create a bloom calendar to visualize the availability of forage throughout the year. This calendar should highlight periods of floral abundance as well as potential gaps in forage availability. Early spring and late fall can be challenging times for urban bees, so particularly note what's available during these seasons.

Supplementing Urban Forage

In some urban areas, particularly those with high densities of buildings and minimal vegetation, natural forage may be insufficient to support a healthy bee colony. In these cases, beekeepers may need to take active steps to supplement available forage. This can include planting bee-friendly flowers, shrubs, and trees on your property or collaborating with neighbors and community groups to create pollinator gardens. Container gardening is also an effective strategy for adding forage on balconies and rooftops. Select plants that bloom at different times of the year to create a continuous food source, focusing on species known for their high nectar and pollen production.

Engaging with Community Initiatives

Urban beekeepers can significantly impact forage availability by engaging with community initiatives aimed at creating pollinator-friendly environments. Participating in or organizing local "plant-a-tree" or "seed bomb" events can help increase the city's overall greenery and forage potential. Working with local governments to advocate for the incorporation of bee-friendly plants in public landscaping projects can also expand the forage landscape for urban bees.

Utilizing Technology and Resources

Leverage technology and available resources to enhance your understanding of local flora and forage. Apps and websites dedicated to pollinator support can offer insights into the best plants for your area and their bloom times. Collaborating with online forums and local beekeeping clubs can also provide tips and firsthand experiences on managing forage in similar urban settings.

Thoroughly assessing your urban environment for local flora and forage availability means you can ensure that your bees not only survive but thrive in the city. This proactive approach to understanding and enhancing the urban landscape for pollinators is a fundamental step in the successful establishment of an urban beekeeping operation.

Choosing Bee Species for Urban Settings

Characteristics of Different Bee Species

When venturing into urban beekeeping, one of the most critical decisions you'll face is selecting the appropriate bee species for your environment. Urban settings, with their unique challenges such as limited space, proximity to humans, and varied foraging options, necessitate careful consideration of the bee species that will thrive under these conditions. Below, we provide an overview of the characteristics of different bee species commonly kept in urban environments, focusing on their traits, behavior, and suitability for the urban beekeeper.

Italian Honey Bee (*Apis mellifera ligustica*)

The Italian honey bee is one of the most popular choices for both novice and experienced beekeepers, and for good reason. These bees are known for their gentle nature, making them less likely to sting, which is a considerable advantage in densely populated urban areas. They are excellent producers of honey and have a relatively low tendency to swarm, reducing the risk of bees escaping into unwanted areas. Additionally, their adaptability to various climates and environments makes them a versatile choice for urban settings.

Carniolan Honey Bee (*Apis mellifera carnica*)

Carniolan honey bees are prized for their ability to forage in cooler temperatures and their excellent sense of orientation, which minimizes their likelihood of getting lost in urban landscapes. They are known for their gentle disposition and are less prone to robbing other hives, a behavior that can spread diseases. Carniolans also have a high tolerance for crowded conditions, making them well-suited for urban environments where space is at a premium. However, their propensity to swarm may require more active swarm management strategies compared to Italian bees.

Caucasian Honey Bee (*Apis mellifera caucasica*)

Caucasian honey bees are valued for their resistance to certain pests and diseases, particularly Varroa mites, which can be a significant advantage in managing hive health without extensive chemical treatments. They are hardy bees, capable of surviving harsh winters and quickly building up their population in the spring. While they can be more defensive than Italian or Carniolan bees, their resilience and lower maintenance health-wise make them a consideration for urban beekeepers willing to manage their more protective nature.

Urban Hybrid Bees

Some urban beekeepers opt for hybrid bees, which are crossbred from different species to enhance certain desirable traits, such as gentleness, productivity, and disease resistance. Hybrids can offer a good balance for urban settings, combining the best characteristics of various species to suit the specific challenges of urban beekeeping. It's important to source these bees from reputable breeders to ensure the desired traits are predominant.

Considerations for Urban Beekeepers

Choosing the right bee species for an urban environment involves balancing productivity, manageability, and adaptability. It's crucial to consider the specific conditions of your urban setting, including climate, available forage, and your proximity to neighbors and public spaces. Additionally, local beekeeping clubs and associations can provide invaluable advice and insights based on their experiences with different bee species in your area.

The choice of bee species is a fundamental decision that can influence the success and enjoyment of urban beekeeping. By understanding the characteristics and needs of different bee species, urban beekeepers can make informed choices that align with their goals, environments, and the well-being of their bee colonies.

Gathering Your Beekeeping Gear

Essential Equipment List

As you embark on your urban beekeeping journey, equipping yourself with the right gear is crucial for both your success and safety. Beekeeping is a hands-on activity that requires specific tools and equipment to manage the hive, ensure your protection, and care for your bees effectively. This section provides a comprehensive checklist of the essential beekeeping gear you'll need to get started. Understanding what is necessary and distinguishing it from optional extras will help streamline your preparation process, ensuring you're well-equipped without unnecessary expenditures.

- **Beehive**: The cornerstone of your beekeeping venture. There are several types of hives, including Langstroth, Top-Bar, and Warre hives, each with its own set of advantages. For urban settings, the Langstroth hive is popular because of its modular design and ease of management. Choose a hive that suits your urban space and beekeeping goals.

- **Protective Clothing**: Beekeeping suits, gloves, and veils are non-negotiable for protecting yourself from stings. A full bee suit or a jacket with a veil can offer varying levels of protection depending on your comfort and the aggressiveness of your bees. Ensure your clothing is light-colored and smooth-textured to be less provocative to bees.

- **Smoker**: A smoker is essential for calming bees during hive inspections or when performing any hive management tasks. Smoke masks alarm pheromones released by guard bees, making them less likely to become agitated and sting.

- **Hive Tools**: A hive tool is an indispensable instrument for any beekeeper. It is used for prying apart hive components, scraping off excess propolis or wax, and lifting frames. The most common types are the standard flat hive tool and the J-hook hive tool.

- **Feeders**: Especially important during the early stages of your hive's development or in times of scarce forage, feeders help supplement your bees' diet. There are various types of feeders, such as entrance feeders, top-hive feeders, and frame feeders. Choose one that best fits your hive's design and your feeding strategy.

- **Bee Brush**: A gentle way to move bees from surfaces without harming them. The bee brush is particularly useful during hive inspections or when harvesting honey, allowing you to clear bees from frames or other areas of the hive with care.

- **Uncapping Tools**: If you plan to harvest honey, uncapping tools are necessary for removing the thin wax layer that seals honey in the cells. Options include uncapping knives (electric or non-electric) and uncapping forks or scratchers.

- **Extractor**: While not immediately essential, an extractor is invaluable when it comes time to harvest honey. Manual extractors are suitable for small-scale urban beekeepers. This tool spins the honey out of the frames using centrifugal force, making the extraction process efficient and preserving the integrity of the comb.

This essential equipment list is your starting point for gathering the gear you'll need for urban beekeeping. While some items may require an initial investment, selecting quality tools and equipment will ensure longevity and reliability, contributing to a more enjoyable and successful beekeeping experience. As you grow in your beekeeping journey, you may find other tools and accessories that suit your specific needs, but these essentials will get you off to a strong start.

Recommendations for Urban-Specific Gear

Urban beekeeping presents a unique set of challenges, not least of which is the proximity to neighbors and the need to efficiently use limited space. Selecting the right equipment is crucial for integrating beekeeping seamlessly into urban environments. This section offers tailored advice on choosing gear that is not only effective but also considerate of the urban context.

Compact and Efficient Hive Designs

One of the first considerations for an urban beekeeper is the selection of a hive design. Traditional hives can be large and may not fit comfortably in smaller urban spaces like balconies or rooftops. Compact hive designs, such as the vertical top-bar hive or modified Langstroth hives, offer a more space-efficient solution. These hives take up less footprint while still providing ample room for your bees to thrive. Look for designs that also offer easy access for management and harvesting, minimizing the disturbance to the bees and the surrounding area.

Noise-Reducing Tools and Equipment

Beekeeping activities can sometimes generate noise, which may be a concern in densely populated areas. Using tools and equipment designed to minimize noise can help maintain good relations with your neighbors. For example, consider investing in a quiet, smokeless bee smoker or electric extractors that feature noise reduction technology. When performing hive inspections or maintenance, using gentle, smooth movements can also significantly reduce disturbance, both to the bees and any nearby residents.

Non-Intrusive Beekeeping Practices

Beyond the physical gear, adopting non-intrusive beekeeping practices is essential in urban settings. This includes scheduling hive inspections during midday when most neighbors are likely to be at work or school, thus minimizing the potential for disturbance. Additionally, positioning your hives away from direct foot traffic and using barriers or screens can help keep bees on a flight path that reduces interactions with humans and pets.

Innovative Forage Solutions

In urban environments, ensuring your bees have access to adequate forage can be challenging. Innovative gear like portable pollinator gardens or flower boxes designed for small spaces can supplement your bees' foraging options. These can be placed on balconies, patios, or rooftops, providing not only a source of nectar and pollen for your bees but also adding aesthetic value to your space.

Protective Gear for Urban Beekeepers

While protective gear is a staple of beekeeping in any setting, urban beekeepers might opt for gear that is less conspicuous. Modern beekeeping suits are available in various colors and styles that blend more naturally into urban surroundings, reducing the visual impact of beekeeping activities. Lightweight and ventilated suits are also more comfortable for the warmer temperatures often found in urban heat islands.

Selecting the right gear for urban beekeeping goes beyond mere functionality. It involves considering the impact on your space, your bees, and your neighbors. By choosing compact, efficient, and non-intrusive equipment, you can ensure your urban beekeeping venture is successful and harmonious, contributing positively to your community and the urban ecosystem.

Navigating Local Regulations and Permissions

For urban beekeepers, the excitement of establishing a hive is often accompanied by the complexity of navigating local regulations and permissions. Urban areas come with a unique set of rules and guidelines designed to ensure that beekeeping activities harmonize with community standards and safety. This section aims to provide a roadmap for understanding and adhering to these local beekeeping regulations, ensuring that your venture into urban beekeeping starts on solid legal ground.

Researching Local Beekeeping Laws

The first step in navigating local regulations is thorough research. Beekeeping laws can vary significantly from one municipality to another, and even within different neighborhoods of the same city. Start by consulting your city or town's official website for any ordinances specifically related to beekeeping. Look for information under zoning laws, animal control regulations, and public health guidelines. If the information isn't readily available online, consider contacting your local government offices directly. They can provide guidance or direct you to the relevant department that oversees beekeeping activities.

Obtaining Necessary Permissions

Once you have a clear understanding of the local laws, the next step is to obtain any necessary permissions. This might involve applying for a beekeeping permit or license, which could require submitting details about your proposed beekeeping setup, including the number of hives, location, and how you plan to manage them. Be prepared to comply with specific requirements, such as maintaining a certain distance between your hives and property lines or implementing measures to manage bee flight paths and provide water for your bees to prevent them from venturing into neighboring areas.

Ensuring Compliance with City Ordinances and HOA Rules

Besides city or municipal regulations, urban beekeepers must also navigate homeowners' association (HOA) rules or apartment building policies. These organizations often have their own set of guidelines regarding activities that can be conducted within their governed properties. Review your HOA's bylaws or speak directly with building management to understand any restrictions or approval processes related to beekeeping. It's essential to secure this approval in writing to avoid any future disputes.

Engaging with Neighbors

A key aspect of navigating local regulations successfully involves engaging with your neighbors. Open communication about your beekeeping activities can help alleviate any concerns and foster a supportive community environment. Share your knowledge about the benefits of urban beekeeping, the measures you're taking to ensure safety, and how you plan to manage the bees responsibly. In some cases, offering a share of the honey produced can sweeten their perception of your beekeeping endeavors.

Staying Informed and Adaptable

Laws and regulations can evolve, so it's important for urban beekeepers to stay informed about any changes that might affect their beekeeping practices. Joining local beekeeping associations or clubs can be invaluable in this regard. These organizations often provide members with updates on local beekeeping laws, advocacy opportunities, and resources for compliance.

Thoroughly researching local laws, obtaining the necessary permissions, and engaging proactively with your community means that you can ensure that your urban beekeeping operation not only complies with legal requirements but also contributes positively to your local environment. Navigating these regulations thoughtfully lays the foundation for a successful and sustainable urban beekeeping practice.

Preparing for Bee Arrival

The anticipation of welcoming bees into their new urban home is both exciting and crucial in the journey of urban beekeeping. Preparing your space for the arrival of bees involves meticulous planning and thoughtful setup to ensure a smooth transition for your pollinators. This section will guide you through the essential steps of setting up the hive, ensuring water availability, and creating an inviting environment for your bees.

Additionally, we'll offer insights on the best timing for introducing bees to their new urban environment.

Setting Up the Hive

The first step in preparing for your bees' arrival is establishing their home—the hive. Choosing the right location within your urban space can make a significant difference in the success of your beekeeping endeavor. Look for a spot that receives morning sun but is shaded during the hottest part of the day, as this can help regulate the temperature inside the hive. Ensure the location is shielded from strong winds, which could destabilize the hive or make it difficult for bees to enter and exit. If possible, position the hive entrance facing south or southeast to maximize sun exposure.

When assembling the hive, follow the manufacturer's instructions carefully. Ensure all components are secure and that the hive stands level on the ground or rooftop. Consider raising the hive off the ground with a sturdy stand or hive legs to protect it from dampness and pests.

Ensuring Water Availability

Bees need a consistent water source not just for drinking but also to regulate the temperature and humidity of their hive. Before your bees arrive, set up a water station near the hive. This can be as simple as a shallow dish filled with pebbles or marbles and water, allowing bees to land safely and drink without drowning. Change the water regularly to keep it clean and prevent mosquitoes from breeding.

Creating an Inviting Environment

Creating an inviting environment for your bees means ensuring they have access to a variety of forage options. Planting bee-friendly flowers, shrubs, and trees that bloom at different times of the year can provide your bees with a continuous source of nectar and pollen. Consider plants like lavender, sage, rosemary, and other native flowers that thrive in your urban area. Additionally, avoid using pesticides or chemicals in your garden or on your balcony, as these can be harmful to bees.

©Anthony Carter | www.beekeeping-101.com | part of Carman Online Content Publishing Ltd

Timing Your Setup

Timing is everything when it comes to introducing bees to their new urban home. The best time to install your bees is in the spring, when flowers begin to bloom, and the weather starts to warm up. This gives your bees ample time to build up their colony strength, store food, and prepare for the winter months. Check with local beekeeping associations for specific recommendations on timing based on your area's climate and forage availability.

By following these steps, you can ensure that your space is well-prepared for the arrival of your bees, setting the stage for a successful and rewarding urban beekeeping experience. Remember, the effort you put into preparing your space will pay off in the health and productivity of your bee colony, contributing positively to your local urban ecosystem.

Conclusion

Embarking on the path of urban beekeeping is a journey filled with learning, growth, and the profound satisfaction of contributing to the ecological health of our cities. The journey, while requiring meticulous planning and preparation, unfolds as an incredibly enriching experience that intertwines the art of beekeeping with the rhythms of urban life. This chapter has laid out the essential steps to get started, paving the way for a successful urban beekeeping venture.

Assessing your urban environment for its beekeeping potential is the critical first step, allowing you to understand the unique challenges and opportunities your specific setting offers. This assessment ensures that your beekeeping practices are in harmony with the surrounding urban ecosystem, promoting the well-being of your bees and the community at large. Following this, selecting the right bee species for your environment is paramount. The choice of species significantly influences your beekeeping experience, impacting everything from hive health to your interaction with the bees.

©Anthony Carter | www.beekeeping-101.com |part of Carman Online Content Publishing Ltd

Equally important is gathering the necessary equipment and supplies, which forms the backbone of your beekeeping operation. This step not only prepares you for the practical aspects of beekeeping, but also reinforces your commitment to providing a safe and productive environment for your bees. Moreover, understanding and adhering to local regulations is essential for integrating your beekeeping practice within the urban fabric, ensuring that your venture is not only successful but also sustainable and community friendly.

This chapter has provided you with the foundational knowledge and tools to start your urban beekeeping adventure with confidence. The journey ahead is not without its challenges, but the rewards of urban beekeeping—enhancing biodiversity, contributing to the pollination of urban flora, and harvesting your own honey—are immeasurable. As you step into the world of urban beekeeping, remember that each hive you establish not only enriches your life but also plays a vital role in the larger effort to sustain urban ecosystems.

With the groundwork now laid, you are well-equipped to move forward in your urban beekeeping journey. The subsequent chapters will build upon this foundation, offering deeper insights into hive management, colony health, and the intricacies of bee behavior, guiding you towards becoming a proficient and responsible urban beekeeper. The adventure of urban beekeeping awaits, promising a rewarding experience as you forge a closer connection with nature right in the heart of the city.

©Anthony Carter | www.beekeeping-101.com |part of Carman Online Content Publishing Ltd

Chapter 3: Legal and Ethical Considerations

In Chapter 3, we delve into the crucial aspects of legal and ethical considerations that every urban beekeeper must navigate to ensure their beekeeping endeavors are both lawful and harmoniously integrated into the urban fabric. As cities become increasingly interested in sustainability and biodiversity, urban beekeeping has emerged as a practice rich with potential benefits yet fraught with unique challenges.

This chapter aims to equip you with the knowledge necessary to comply with local regulations, foster positive relationships with your community, and adhere to ethical beekeeping practices. By understanding and respecting the legal frameworks, engaging constructively with neighbors, and prioritizing the welfare of your bees and the local ecosystem, you can establish a beekeeping practice that is not only successful but also sustainable and welcomed in an urban setting.

Understanding and Complying with Local Regulations

Navigating Local Laws and Ordinances

Urban beekeeping, while rewarding, requires a careful approach to legal compliance. The first step for any aspiring or current urban beekeeper is to thoroughly understand the local beekeeping laws, which can significantly differ from one city to another, or even between neighborhoods within the same city. This variability means that what is permissible in one area may be restricted or require specific conditions to be met in another.

Where to Find Relevant Information:

- **City Council Websites:** Many city or municipal websites have a section dedicated to local bylaws and ordinances, including those related to beekeeping. These resources are invaluable for understanding the specific legal framework within your city.

- **Local Beekeeping Associations:** Joining a local beekeeping association can provide access to a wealth of knowledge about the nuances of beekeeping laws in your area. These associations often offer workshops, meetings, and forums where members can share advice and experiences related to legal compliance.
- **Agricultural Extension Offices:** Extension offices are a resource for the agricultural community, providing information on a wide range of topics, including beekeeping. They can offer guidance on state and local regulations, as well as best practices for urban beekeeping.

Common Regulatory Considerations:

When researching local laws, there are several key areas you'll need to consider to ensure your beekeeping operation complies with all legal requirements. These include:

- **Hive Density Limits:** Some areas restrict the number of hives you can keep based on the size of your property. This is to prevent overcrowding and ensure bees have adequate access to forage.
- **Location Restrictions:** There may be regulations specifying how far hives must be placed from property lines, dwellings, and public spaces. Such rules are designed to minimize potential conflicts with neighbors and pedestrians.
- **Permit Requirements:** Depending on your location, you might need to apply for a permit or license to keep bees. This process can involve submitting an application, paying a fee, and sometimes undergoing an inspection of your proposed beekeeping site.

Checklist for Legal Compliance:

To assist you in navigating the legal landscape of urban beekeeping, consider the following checklist:

- **Research Local Ordinances:** Check your city or municipal website and consult with local beekeeping associations for the most current regulations.

- **Understand Hive Placement Rules:** Make sure you know any specific requirements for hive placement to avoid potential issues with neighbors or the city.
- **Check for Permit Requirements:** Find out if you need a permit to keep bees and what the application process involves.
- **Stay Informed About Changes:** Laws and regulations can change, so it's important to stay informed through local beekeeping associations and city council updates.

Taking the time to thoroughly understand and comply with local regulations means you can ensure your urban beekeeping practice not only thrives but also contributes positively to your community and the environment. This proactive approach to legal compliance will set the foundation for a successful and sustainable urban beekeeping endeavor.

Permits, Inspections, and Insurance

Urban beekeeping, while rewarding, involves navigating a series of legal requirements to ensure that your activities are in full compliance with local laws and ordinances. This section outlines the essential steps for obtaining necessary permits or licenses, preparing for hive inspections, and securing liability insurance, all of which are pivotal in establishing and maintaining a lawful and responsible urban beekeeping practice.

Applying for Permits or Licenses

- **Research Local Requirements:** Begin by thoroughly researching your city or municipality's specific beekeeping laws. This can typically be done by visiting official city websites, contacting local beekeeping associations, or consulting with the department of agriculture or environmental protection in your area.
- **Understand the Specifics:** Pay close attention to the details of the regulations, such as the number of hives allowed, distance from property lines, and any requirements for signage or barriers.
- **Prepare Your Application:** Collect any necessary documentation, which may include a detailed plan of your beekeeping setup, a site

map of your property showing the location of hives, and possibly a letter of intent outlining your beekeeping goals and how you plan to manage your bees responsibly.

- **Submit Application and Fee:** Complete the required application forms and submit them, along with any applicable fees, to the appropriate regulatory body. Be prepared for a waiting period as your application is reviewed.

Hive Inspections

- **Preparation:** Once your permit is granted, your hives may be subject to periodic inspections by local authorities to ensure compliance with health, safety, and welfare standards. Prepare for inspections by maintaining detailed records of your beekeeping practices, including hive health, pest management strategies, and any treatments applied.
- **Understanding Inspection Criteria:** Inspectors will typically check for signs of disease or pests, the general health of the bee colony, and the safety of the hive's location in relation to public spaces and neighboring properties.
- **Following Up:** If issues are identified during an inspection, you will be given instructions on how to address them. Promptly following up on these recommendations is crucial to remain in compliance and to ensure the health and safety of your bees and the surrounding community.

Obtaining Liability Insurance

- **Assessing Your Needs:** Liability insurance is an essential consideration for urban beekeepers. It protects you in the event that your bees cause harm or damage to someone or their property.
- **Researching Options:** Contact insurance providers to discuss options for coverage. Some homeowner's insurance policies may offer add-ons for beekeeping activities, or you may need to seek a specific policy designed for agricultural or beekeeping activities.

- **Comparing Coverage:** Ensure that the insurance policy covers the key risks associated with beekeeping, including bee stings, hive theft or vandalism, and damage to third-party property.
- **Finalizing Your Policy:** Once you've selected a policy that meets your needs, complete the application process, and keep your policy up to date. Regularly review and adjust your coverage as your beekeeping operation grows or changes.

If you diligently follow these steps for permits, inspections, and insurance, you can establish a foundation for your urban beekeeping practice that respects legal requirements, prioritizes the health and safety of your bees, and minimizes risk to yourself and your community. This proactive approach not only ensures compliance, but also contributes to the positive perception and success of urban beekeeping initiatives.

Engaging with Neighbors and the Community

Communicating with Neighbors

For urban beekeepers, fostering a positive relationship with neighbors is as crucial as the care for the bees themselves. Transparent communication and educational outreach can transform skepticism into support, ensuring your beekeeping endeavors enhance the community. Here's how to approach this vital aspect of urban beekeeping:

Introducing the Topic

- **Personal Conversations**: Begin by informally discussing your beekeeping plans with your neighbors. A personal conversation allows for a direct exchange of thoughts and concerns, making it easier to address any misunderstandings about beekeeping.
- **Highlighting Benefits**: Explain the critical role bees play in pollinating local gardens and green spaces, leading to more abundant flora and a healthier ecosystem. Emphasize how urban beekeeping contributes to biodiversity and urban food production.

Addressing Concerns

- **Safety and Allergies**: Address common worries about bee stings and allergies by explaining the nature of bee behavior, the non-aggressive temperament of certain bee species, and the measures you'll take to position hives thoughtfully to minimize interactions.
- **Education on Bee Behavior**: Offer insights into bee behavior, noting that bees are generally not interested in humans unless provoked. Share how proper hive management reduces the likelihood of negative encounters.

Creating Informative Materials

- **Flyers and Newsletters**: Design simple yet informative flyers or newsletters that outline the benefits of urban beekeeping, interesting facts about bees, and how you plan to manage your hives responsibly. Include contact information for neighbors to reach out with questions or concerns.
- **FAQ Section**: Anticipate and answer common questions in your materials. This could cover topics like what happens if a bee stings someone, how you'll manage the hive during different seasons, and the steps you're taking to ensure the bees are a positive addition to the neighborhood.

Highlighting the Benefits of Having Bees in the Neighborhood

- **Environmental Impact**: Detail how urban bees aid in pollinating local plants, which can lead to more lush gardens and possibly even improve yields for home vegetable growers.
- **Community Engagement**: Mention any plans for community involvement, such as educational workshops, honey tastings, or open days for neighbors to learn more about beekeeping. This can help demystify beekeeping and show its value to the community.
- **Sharing the Harvest**: Offer to share honey with the community or propose creating products like beeswax candles or lip balms as small tokens of appreciation. This tangible benefit can help

neighbors feel directly invested in the success of your beekeeping project.

Effective communication with neighbors not only alleviates concerns, but also builds a community of informed and supportive individuals. By taking these steps, you can help ensure that your urban beekeeping initiative is welcomed and that your bees become a valued part of the neighborhood ecosystem.

Building Positive Relationships

Fostering positive relationships with your neighbors and the wider community is pivotal for the success and acceptance of your urban beekeeping endeavors. The presence of bees can evoke a range of reactions, from curiosity and enthusiasm to concern and apprehension. Here are strategies to build understanding, trust, and support for your beekeeping activities, ensuring a harmonious coexistence within your urban community.

Inviting Neighbors to Visit Your Hives

One of the most effective ways to demystify beekeeping and dispel fears is to invite neighbors to see your hives up close. Such visits can be informal or part of a planned open house event where you:

- **Demonstrate Beekeeping Tasks:** Show how you inspect hives, explain what you're looking for, and discuss how bees contribute to the environment.
- **Educate on Bee Behavior:** Explain the non-aggressive nature of bees when managed properly and the importance of not swatting or disturbing the bees unnecessarily.
- **Provide Safety Tips:** Offer advice on how to behave around bees and what to do in the unlikely event of a bee sting.

©Anthony Carter | www.beekeeping-101.com |part of Carman Online Content Publishing Ltd

Offering Honey Samples

Sharing the fruits of your labor is a tangible way to connect your neighbors to your beekeeping practice. Honey harvested from urban hives has the unique appeal of being locally produced, and its taste can vary based on the local flora:

- **Package Small Honey Samples:** Small jars of honey can be a delightful gift that introduces neighbors to the quality and flavor of local, raw honey.
- **Include Informational Tags:** Attach tags or small cards that explain the source of the honey, its unique local flavors, and a note about the importance of bees.

Hosting Educational Sessions on Beekeeping and Pollination

Education plays a crucial role in transforming skepticism into support. By hosting educational sessions, you can inform your community about the critical role bees play in our ecosystem and how urban beekeeping can be conducted safely and responsibly:

- **Organize Workshops or Talks:** Cover topics such as the basics of beekeeping, the role of bees in pollination, and how urban beekeeping benefits local gardens and biodiversity.
- **Collaborate with Local Experts:** Invite local beekeepers, entomologists, or environmental educators to speak, providing diverse perspectives and deepening the educational experience.
- **Use Visual Aids:** Employ presentations, handouts, and live demonstrations (if possible) to engage and inform attendees effectively.

Handling Complaints and Concerns with Empathy and Professionalism

Despite your best efforts, some neighbors may still have concerns or complaints about your beekeeping activities. Addressing these issues promptly and empathetically is crucial:

- **Listen Actively:** Give your neighbors a platform to express their concerns, showing that you take their apprehensions seriously.
- **Provide Reassuring Information:** Many fears about bees stem from misconceptions. Offer factual information about bee behavior, hive management, and safety measures you've implemented.
- **Offer Solutions:** If specific concerns are raised, discuss possible solutions or compromises. This could include relocating hives within your property to minimize disturbance or adjusting your beekeeping schedule to less active times in the community.

Embracing these strategies means you can foster a positive and inclusive atmosphere around your urban beekeeping practice. Building relationships based on respect, education, and open communication ensures that beekeeping becomes a valued part of the urban community, enriching the local environment and fostering a deeper connection with nature.

Ethical Urban Beekeeping Practices

Responsible Hive Management

At the heart of ethical urban beekeeping lies the commitment to responsible hive management. This section focuses on the importance of selecting appropriate hive locations, maintaining healthy bee populations, and implementing sustainable practices that benefit both the bees and the urban community.

Choosing Hive Locations with Care

Minimizing Disturbance to Neighbors

- Selecting a hive location goes beyond finding a spot in your yard; it involves considering the impact on your neighbors and the surrounding community. Try to opt for locations that are discreet, away from high foot traffic, and shielded by barriers or vegetation to prevent direct interaction with people and pets.

- Orienting the hive entrance away from neighboring properties and public spaces can significantly reduce the chance of bees flying into human activity areas, thus minimizing potential concerns or fears from neighbors.

Ensuring Adequate Access to Forage

- The placement of your hives should also take into account the availability of forage throughout the year. Urban beekeepers must assess their environment for sources of nectar and pollen, ensuring bees have access to a variety of flowering plants within flying distance.
- Engage in creating or supporting urban green spaces that can serve as forage sites for your bees. Collaborate with local authorities, community gardens, and neighbors to enhance the floral diversity in your area, benefiting not just your bees but the entire urban ecosystem.

Maintaining Healthy Bee Populations

Regular Health Checks and Monitoring

- The cornerstone of responsible hive management is the commitment to regular and thorough health inspections of your colonies. These checks allow for early detection of diseases, pests, and other stress factors that could affect your bees' health and productivity.
- Implement a routine schedule for inspecting your hives, paying close attention to the queen's health, brood pattern, and signs of diseases or parasites. Keep detailed records of your observations to track the colony's health over time.

Sustainable Pest Management Strategies

- Addressing pests and diseases in an urban setting requires a careful balance between effectiveness and environmental impact. Choose integrated pest management (IPM) strategies that prioritize

mechanical, cultural, and biological controls over chemical interventions.
- When chemical treatments are necessary, choose products that are least harmful to bees, other pollinators, and the environment. Always follow label instructions and consider the timing of applications to minimize exposure to the colony.

Avoiding Overcrowding of Hives

- Overcrowding can lead to increased stress on bees, heightened aggression, and the potential for swarming, which could raise concerns among urban residents. Monitor your hives' population density and be prepared to split colonies or provide additional space when necessary.
- Educate yourself on swarm prevention techniques and have a plan in place to capture and re-home swarms safely should they occur. This not only prevents potential conflicts with neighbors but also provides an opportunity to expand your apiary or support other urban beekeepers.

Responsible hive management is at the core of ethical urban beekeeping. By carefully considering the location of your hives, ensuring access to diverse forage, conducting regular health inspections, employing sustainable pest management, and preventing overcrowding, you can foster a thriving urban apiary. These practices not only safeguard the health and well-being of your bees, but also contribute positively to the community and the urban environment, embodying the true spirit of ethical beekeeping.

Ensuring Bee Health and Welfare

In the context of urban beekeeping, prioritizing the health and welfare of your bee colonies goes beyond mere hive management—it's about making ethical decisions that benefit both the bees and the urban ecosystem they inhabit. This section focuses on the importance of bee species selection

©Anthony Carter | www.beekeeping-101.com | part of Carman Online Content Publishing Ltd

and forage diversity, as well as the implementation of stress-minimizing techniques, to promote thriving, healthy bee populations in the city.

Selecting Bee Varieties Suited to Urban Environments

Choosing the right bee species is a foundational step in urban beekeeping. Not all bees are equally suited to the conditions found in city environments, where space is limited and foraging options may vary significantly from rural settings. Some bee varieties are more adaptable to smaller spaces, have gentler temperaments, making them less of a concern for neighbors, or are more efficient at foraging over longer distances, which is crucial in urban areas where green spaces are scattered.

- **Research and Consultation:** Start by researching bee species known for their adaptability to urban life. Consult local beekeeping clubs and extension services for recommendations on bee varieties that thrive in your specific climate and urban landscape.
- **Temperament and Foraging Range:** Consider gentle bee species that are less likely to be perceived as a threat by urban residents. Species with a broader foraging range can better adapt to the patchy availability of forage in cities.

Providing a Diverse Range of Forage

Urban beekeepers must ensure their bees have access to a consistent and diverse range of forage throughout the blooming season. This diversity is crucial for bee nutrition, immunity, and overall colony health. In urban settings, where natural forage can be limited or seasonal, beekeepers can take proactive steps to enhance the foraging landscape.

- **Planting Bee-Friendly Flora:** Whether in your garden, on your balcony, or in community green spaces, prioritize planting native and non-invasive plants that offer a succession of blooms from early spring to late fall. This helps provide bees with a continuous source of nectar and pollen.
- **Collaboration for Green Spaces:** Work with local community gardens, parks, and other urban green spaces to promote the

©Anthony Carter | www.beekeeping-101.com | part of Carman Online Content Publishing Ltd

planting of bee-friendly vegetation. Advocating for urban planning that includes green corridors and pollinator gardens can significantly improve foraging options for urban bees.

Minimizing Stress and Promoting Wellbeing

The well-being of bees in urban settings is closely tied to how they are managed and interacted with by the beekeeper. Stress reduction is key to maintaining healthy colonies.

- **Gentle Handling During Inspections:** Use smooth, calm movements when inspecting hives to avoid agitating the bees. Minimize the frequency of inspections to necessary checks for health, space, and resources, ensuring each inspection is as quick and efficient as possible.
- **Avoiding the Use of Harsh Chemicals:** Whenever possible, go for natural, organic methods of pest and disease management. Many chemical treatments can harm bees or reduce their resilience. Integrated pest management (IPM) strategies that focus on preventive measures and minimal intervention can be effective in urban beekeeping without the need for harsh chemicals.

If you adopt these practices, as an urban beekeeper you can ensure your hives not only survive but thrive in city environments. Ethical beekeeping practices that prioritize bee health and welfare contribute to the sustainability of urban beekeeping and the broader goal of supporting urban ecosystems.

Contributing to Urban Ecology

As urban beekeepers, we have a unique opportunity to positively impact the urban ecology beyond the confines of our hives. Our practices can contribute significantly to the enhancement of urban biodiversity and the support of local ecosystems. This section explores how urban beekeepers can extend their influence on the broader urban environment, focusing on planting native and bee-friendly flora and engaging in public education and advocacy for pollinator-friendly urban policies.

Planting Native and Bee-Friendly Flora

Creating Pollinator Havens in Urban Spaces

- Urban areas often lack the diversity of plants necessary to support healthy pollinator populations. Beekeepers can transform spaces, no matter how small, into thriving habitats for bees by planting native and bee-friendly plants. Balconies, rooftops, community gardens, and even window boxes can serve as valuable foraging sites.
- Tips for selecting plants: Focus on native species that thrive in your area, as these will provide the most nutritional benefits to your bees and require less maintenance. Choose a variety of plants that bloom at different times of the year to ensure a consistent food source for bees.

The Benefits of Diverse Urban Foraging Options

- A diverse planting strategy not only benefits your bees by providing a rich source of nectar and pollen, but also supports other local pollinators. This diversity enhances the resilience of urban ecosystems, making them more robust against environmental pressures and challenges.
- Encourage local community efforts: Collaborate with neighbors, schools, and community groups to create larger pollinator-friendly spaces. Such initiatives can transform urban areas into interconnected habitats, offering extensive foraging opportunities for bees and other pollinators.

Educating the Public and Advocacy

Raising Awareness Among Urban Dwellers

- Many city residents are unaware of the critical role pollinators play in our ecosystems and food supply. Urban beekeepers are in a prime position to educate the public about the importance of bees through workshops, school programs, and community events. Sharing knowledge about the benefits of bees can help ease fears and misconceptions, fostering a community that values and protects these essential insects.

Advocating for Pollinator-Friendly Urban Policies

- Urban beekeepers can serve as advocates for policies that support pollinators, such as the creation of green spaces, the planting of bee-friendly vegetation in public areas, and the reduction of pesticide use. By engaging with local government and taking part in urban planning processes, beekeepers can help shape a more sustainable and pollinator-friendly urban landscape.
- Strategies for effective advocacy include joining or forming local beekeeping associations, collaborating with environmental groups, and using social media and other platforms to raise awareness and influence policy.

Contributing to urban ecology is a critical component of ethical urban beekeeping. By planting native and bee-friendly flora, urban beekeepers can enhance the availability of foraging resources for bees, supporting not only their hives but also the broader community of urban pollinators. Additionally, by educating the public about the importance of pollinators and advocating for supportive urban policies, beekeepers can play a pivotal role in fostering a more sustainable and pollinator-friendly urban environment. This proactive approach to beekeeping extends the impact of our hives into the community, promoting biodiversity and ecological health in our urban spaces.

Conclusion

As we conclude Chapter 3, it's clear that the path to successful urban beekeeping is paved with more than just good intentions and a love for bees. The intricate dance between legal obligations, community relations, and ethical stewardship forms the backbone of a practice that extends far beyond hobby or passion—it becomes a testament to our commitment to sustainability, biodiversity, and the well-being of our urban environments. This chapter has laid out the foundational steps for navigating the legal landscape, building bridges with neighbors and the wider community, and embodying the ethics of care and responsibility that should guide every urban beekeeper's actions.

Legal compliance is not merely a bureaucratic hurdle; it's a framework within which we ensure our beekeeping practices align with the collective standards and safety of our communities. Engaging with neighbors and the community isn't just about mitigating complaints; it's an opportunity to educate, share, and spread the enthusiasm for bees and their critical role in our ecosystems. And ethical beekeeping practices are not just about the health of our hives; they reflect our broader responsibility to the environment and the future of urban ecology.

By adhering to these principles, urban beekeepers don't just navigate the complexities of their craft; they become ambassadors for bees in the urban landscape, advocates for sustainability, and contributors to the environmental health of their communities. The journey of urban beekeeping is one of continuous learning, adaptation, and engagement. As we move forward, let's carry the insights from this chapter with us, fostering a sustainable coexistence between urban life and the vital pollinators that enrich our world in countless ways. Together, we can ensure that urban beekeeping remains a force for good, for the bees, for our communities, and for the planet.

©Anthony Carter | www.beekeeping-101.com | part of Carman Online Content Publishing Ltd

Chapter 4: Hive Management in Limited Spaces

Urban beekeeping presents a unique set of challenges, particularly when it comes to managing hives in the confined spaces typical of city environments. The limitations imposed by smaller living areas, proximity to neighbors, and the need for safety and accessibility make traditional beekeeping methods a poor fit for urban settings. However, with the right approach and innovative thinking, these challenges can be turned into opportunities.

This chapter delves into the essential aspects of urban hive management, offering guidance on selecting the best locations for your hives within city confines, introducing hive designs that are both efficient and space-saving, and outlining the maintenance practices crucial for the health and productivity of urban bee colonies. By adapting to the constraints of urban living and adopting practices tailored for smaller spaces, beekeepers can ensure their hives not only survive but thrive, contributing positively to urban ecosystems and the broader community. Through careful planning and consideration, urban beekeeping becomes not just a possibility but a rewarding endeavor, bringing the joys and benefits of beekeeping to the heart of the city.

Selecting the Perfect Spot for Your Hive

Evaluating Urban Spaces for Bees

Choosing the right location for your urban beehive is crucial for the health and productivity of your bee colony. Urban environments offer unique challenges and opportunities for beekeeping, and understanding how to effectively evaluate potential hive sites is the first step towards successful urban beekeeping. This section will guide you through the key factors to consider when selecting a location for your hive, ensuring your bees thrive in their new home.

Importance of Sunlight Exposure and Wind Protection

Bees need a warm and stable environment to thrive, making sunlight exposure and protection from the wind critical considerations when selecting a hive location. A spot that receives morning sunlight can help to warm the bees early in the day, encouraging them to start their foraging activities. However, it's also important to ensure that the hive is not exposed to intense midday heat, which can stress the colony. Look for locations that offer a balance of sun and shade to keep the hive temperature consistent.

Wind protection is equally important, as strong winds can cool the hive, making it difficult for bees to maintain the necessary temperature for brood rearing and can even lead to hive damage. Barriers such as walls, hedges, or fences can provide necessary windbreaks, ensuring your bees are protected from harsh weather conditions.

Considering Flight Paths and Pedestrian Traffic

The flight path of bees entering and exiting the hive should be a major consideration in urban settings. Ideally, hives should be positioned so that bees fly at a height above human head level to avoid interactions with pedestrians and neighbors. This can often be achieved by placing hives on rooftops, elevated platforms, or behind barriers that direct the bees' flight upward. It's important to minimize the risk of bee-human interactions to keep both bees and people safe and comfortable with the presence of the hive.

Accessibility for Maintenance and Emergency Access

Regular maintenance and inspection are essential for healthy bee colonies, so ease of access to your hive is a must. Ensure that the location you choose allows for safe and convenient inspections, including during adverse weather conditions. Consider how you will transport equipment and harvested honey to and from the hive site.

Emergency access is also a critical consideration. In the event of a hive issue that requires immediate attention, such as aggressive behavior or disease outbreak, you need to be able to reach and manage the hive quickly and safely. Ensure that the path to your hive is clear and accessible at all times.

Selecting the perfect spot for your hive in an urban environment involves a careful balance of factors. By prioritizing the needs of your bees and considering the impact on your human neighbors, you can identify a location that supports the health and productivity of your bee colony while integrating harmoniously into the urban landscape.

Rooftop Beekeeping Considerations

Rooftop beekeeping has become a popular choice for urban beekeepers, offering a way to utilize often under-used space in densely populated areas. However, setting up hives on a rooftop requires careful planning and consideration of several factors to ensure the safety and productivity of the bee colonies.

Structural Weight Limits and Safety Barriers

Before installing hives on a rooftop, it's crucial to assess the structural integrity of the building. The weight of beehives, especially when full of bees, honey, and equipment, can be significant. Consulting with a structural engineer can help determine if your roof can support the weight of your beekeeping operation. Additionally, installing safety barriers around your hives is essential to protect both the bees and people. These barriers can also serve as windbreaks, providing a more stable environment for the bees.

Benefits of Rooftop Environments for Bees

Rooftop environments offer unique advantages for bees. Elevated from the ground level, hives are often safer from predators and can have reduced exposure to pests. The height can also facilitate a cleaner flight path for foraging bees, potentially leading to healthier colonies. Furthermore, rooftops can mimic natural cliff-side habitats for certain bee species, making them ideal locations for hives.

Challenges and Solutions for Rooftop Access and Water Provision

One of the primary challenges of rooftop beekeeping is ensuring easy and safe access for routine maintenance and inspections. It's important to create a pathway that allows the beekeeper to transport equipment and harvested honey with minimal difficulty. This might involve installing stable walkways or ensuring secure ladder access.

Water provision is another critical consideration. Bees need a consistent water source, especially in urban areas where natural sources may be scarce. Setting up a water station near the hives can prevent bees from seeking water in neighboring swimming pools or other less ideal locations. This station can be as simple as a shallow container filled with water and marbles or pebbles for the bees to land on.

If you address these considerations, rooftop beekeeping can be a highly rewarding and effective way to practice urban beekeeping. It not only optimizes unused space, but also contributes to the biodiversity and health of urban environments. With proper planning and care, rooftop hives can thrive, offering a sanctuary for bees in the city.

Balcony and Backyard Beekeeping

When embarking on the journey of urban beekeeping, the balcony or backyard often presents itself as an appealing option for many city dwellers. These spaces, though limited, can be optimized to create a conducive environment for bees while coexisting peacefully with human residents. This section explores effective strategies for utilizing balconies and backyards for beekeeping, focusing on space optimization, enhancing privacy and safety, and fostering a bee-friendly atmosphere.

Space Optimization Strategies

Maximizing the use of available space is crucial in balcony and backyard beekeeping. To achieve this, consider the following:

- **Vertical Gardening:** Utilize vertical space by installing shelving or hanging gardens that can host a variety of flowering plants. This not only saves space but also provides forage for your bees.
- **Multi-functional Hive Stands:** Design or select hive stands that double as storage for beekeeping equipment. This approach ensures that tools are handy while conserving space.
- **Compact Hive Placement:** Arrange your hives strategically to allow for easy access for maintenance and inspection, ensuring there's sufficient space between them for bees to fly freely without obstruction.

Privacy Screens and Bee-Friendly Plants

Creating a space that respects the privacy of both the bees and your neighbors is essential. Consider these additions:

- **Privacy Screens:** Install lattice screens or tall plants around your beekeeping area to create a visual barrier. This can help direct bee flight patterns upwards and away from human activity, reducing the chance of bee-human encounters.
- **Bee-Friendly Plants:** Select plants that thrive in your local climate and offer abundant nectar and pollen. Lavender, thyme, and rosemary are excellent choices for balconies and backyards, providing forage for bees while adding aesthetic value to your space.

Managing Bees in Close Proximity to Human Activity

Keeping bees close to human living spaces requires careful management to ensure safety and minimize disturbances:

- **Water Sources:** Provide water sources for your bees close to their hives to prevent them from venturing into neighboring areas in search of water. A shallow dish with pebbles or floating wood pieces can serve as an ideal drinking spot.
- **Hive Orientation:** Position the hive entrance facing away from your living areas and neighboring properties. This encourages bees to fly in a direction that minimizes interaction with humans.
- **Regular Monitoring:** Keep a close eye on bee behavior, especially during peak activity periods. Being proactive in managing your hive's health and temperament can prevent issues before they arise.

Balcony and backyard beekeeping, with the right approach, can be immensely satisfying and productive. By optimizing space, ensuring privacy, and creating a bee-friendly environment, urban beekeepers can successfully manage hives in close proximity to human activity. This not only supports the health and productivity of bee colonies, but also fosters a harmonious relationship between bees and people in the urban landscape.

Innovative Hive Designs for Small Spaces

Vertical Hive Options

In the realm of urban beekeeping, where every square inch counts, vertical hive options have emerged as a game-changer. These designs capitalize on the vertical space available, allowing beekeepers to maintain healthy colonies in compact areas. This section explores the advantages of vertical stacking, introduces popular vertical hive models, and provides

©Anthony Carter | www.beekeeping-101.com | part of Carman Online Content Publishing Ltd

customization tips to help urban beekeepers maximize their limited space efficiently.

Advantages of Vertical Stacking in Urban Settings

Vertical stacking offers several key benefits for urban beekeepers:

- **Space Efficiency:** By expanding upwards rather than outwards, vertical hives make the most of small footprints on rooftops, balconies, or backyards.
- **Scalability:** Beekeepers can easily add or remove hive components (like supers for honey storage or brood boxes for colony expansion) depending on the colony's needs and the season, without requiring additional ground space.
- **Accessibility:** Vertical hives are designed for ease of access, making hive inspections and maintenance tasks less physically demanding and more suited to the confined spaces of urban environments.

Overview of Popular Vertical Hive Models

Two vertical hive models stand out for their adaptability to urban settings: the Langstroth and the Warre.

- **Langstroth Hives:** Revered for their modularity, Langstroth hives consist of vertically stackable boxes, each containing frames for the bees to build their comb. This design facilitates easy inspection and honey extraction with minimal disturbance to the bees. The ability to add or subtract boxes based on colony size and honey production makes it a favorite among urban beekeepers.
- **Warre Hives:** Designed to mimic the natural vertical space of a tree hollow, Warre hives offer a more hands-off approach to beekeeping. They feature stackable boxes similar to the Langstroth but are designed to be added at the bottom, encouraging natural comb building from the top down. This model is appreciated for its simplicity and appeal to beekeepers favoring a more naturalistic approach.

Customization Tips for Maximizing Space and Efficiency

Urban beekeeping demands creativity to overcome spatial constraints. Here are some customization tips for vertical hives that can help urban beekeepers optimize their setup:

- **Use of Rooftop Anchor Points:** Securely anchor your hives to rooftop structures to protect them from high winds, leveraging vertical space safely and effectively.
- **Modular Frame Options:** Experiment with different frame sizes and configurations within the hive boxes to maximize honey production and brood space according to your colony's needs.
- **Insulation and Weatherproofing:** Customize your hives with insulation and weatherproofing to protect against the urban heat island effect and ensure your bees remain comfortable throughout the seasons.
- **Integrated Water Sources:** Add small, shallow water sources on or near your hives to provide bees with easy access to water, reducing their need to venture far in search of it.

Embracing vertical hive options and tailoring them to fit the unique conditions of urban environments means that beekeepers can enjoy the satisfaction of beekeeping within the city's constraints. These innovative designs not only accommodate the spatial limitations of urban settings but also contribute to the health and productivity of bee colonies, ensuring their vital role in urban ecosystems continues to thrive.

Compact Hive Innovations

In the quest to adapt beekeeping to urban environments, compact and modular hive designs have emerged as a game-changer. These innovative structures are specifically engineered to address the spatial limitations of city living, offering urban beekeepers practical solutions to keep bees in smaller areas such as balconies, patios, and rooftops. This section explores the world of compact hive innovations, highlighting their design principles, benefits for educational purposes, and strategies for adapting traditional hives to fit into reduced spaces.

Introduction to Compact and Modular Hive Designs

Compact and modular hive designs represent a significant departure from the conventional hive structures used in rural and suburban settings. These designs prioritize space efficiency, modularity, and ease of management, making them ideal for the urban beekeeper. Key features include stackable frames, reduced footprint, and lightweight materials that facilitate easy relocation and management. Some compact hives also offer innovative ventilation systems, removable panels, and clear sections for observation, enhancing the urban beekeeping experience without compromising the health and productivity of the colony.

Benefits of Using Observation Hives in Educational Settings

Observation hives take the concept of compact design a step further by incorporating glass or clear plastic panels that allow beekeepers and the public to view the inner workings of the hive without disturbance. These hives serve as powerful educational tools, especially in urban settings where people may be less familiar with beekeeping and the vital role bees play in our ecosystem. Schools, libraries, and community centers can use observation hives to foster interest in entomology, ecology, and conservation, providing a hands-on learning experience that demystifies bees and promotes conservation efforts.

Adapting Traditional Hive Designs for Small Spaces

While compact and modular hives offer innovative solutions, many urban beekeepers may start with or prefer traditional hive designs, like Langstroth or Top-Bar hives. Adapting these designs for urban settings involves several modifications to reduce their spatial footprint and make them more suitable for limited spaces. Techniques include using fewer frames, customizing the hive's height or width, and incorporating vertical expansion options to encourage upward colony growth rather than outward spread. By customizing traditional hives, urban beekeepers can enjoy the familiarity of conventional beekeeping practices while accommodating the constraints of city living.

In conclusion, compact hive innovations provide urban beekeepers with the tools needed to overcome the challenges of limited space, offering efficient, practical, and educational opportunities to engage with beekeeping in city environments. Whether opting for a modern compact design, using an observation hive for educational purposes, or adapting traditional hives to fit smaller spaces, urban beekeepers can find effective solutions to maintain healthy, productive colonies in the heart of the city.

Creative Placement and Installation

Urban beekeeping often requires thinking outside the box—literally and figuratively—when it comes to hive placement and installation. The limited space of an urban environment encourages beekeepers to explore unconventional locations that can support healthy, productive hives. This exploration not only maximizes the limited space available, but also integrates beekeeping seamlessly into the urban landscape. Here, we delve into strategies for creative hive placement, important safety considerations, and how to blend beekeeping with urban green initiatives like roof gardens and green spaces.

Utilizing Unconventional Spaces for Hive Placement

Urban beekeepers have successfully installed hives in a variety of unconventional spaces, demonstrating that almost any area can become a potential home for bees with the right adjustments. Examples include:

- **Rooftops of residential and commercial buildings:** These spaces are often under-used and can provide a safe, secluded area for hives away from ground-level disturbances.
- **Balconies and terraces:** With careful planning to ensure safety and manage space efficiently, balconies can host small hives, bringing pollinators close to home.

- **Community gardens and parks:** Installing hives in these green spaces not only benefits the bees but also enhances the pollination of local plants, benefiting the entire community.

Safety Considerations and Installation Tips

When installing hives in unconventional spaces, safety is paramount—not just for the beekeeper and the bees, but also for the public. Here are some key considerations:

- **Ensure structural stability:** Especially for rooftop hives, confirm that the structure can support the weight of the hive, particularly when it's full of bees, honey, and wax.
- **Secure hives against elements:** Wind, rain, and extreme temperatures can affect hive stability and health. Secure hives to their bases and provide adequate shelter and insulation.
- **Access routes:** Ensure safe and discreet access for maintenance and emergency situations, minimizing disturbance to the bees and the public.

Incorporating Green Roofs and Garden Designs with Beekeeping in Mind

Green roofs and urban gardens offer a dual benefit of supporting bee populations while enhancing urban biodiversity. Integrating beekeeping into these spaces requires a symbiotic approach:

- **Selecting bee-friendly plants:** Choose a variety of flowering plants that bloom at different times of the year to provide a continuous food source for the bees.
- **Designing with bees in mind:** Arrange garden elements to facilitate bee activity and safety, such as providing clear flight paths and avoiding high-traffic pedestrian areas.
- **Water sources:** Ensure there are safe water sources for bees to hydrate, such as shallow dishes with stones or floating materials for bees to land on.

Creative hive placement and thoughtful integration into urban green spaces not only addresses the challenge of limited space but also contributes to the sustainability and ecological health of urban environments. By considering safety, structural requirements, and the benefits of green roofs and gardens, urban beekeepers can create thriving havens for bees that enrich the urban landscape and foster a closer connection between city dwellers and the natural world.

Maintaining Your Urban Hive

Routine Inspection and Maintenance Tips

Successful urban beekeeping hinges on regular hive inspections and proper maintenance. These practices are vital for the early detection of issues and ensuring the health and productivity of your bee colonies. In the unique context of urban environments, where space is at a premium and beekeeping activities are closely integrated into community spaces, maintaining your hive becomes not just a matter of bee health, but also of public safety and neighborhood relations. This section outlines the frequency of inspections, key indicators of hive health, tools and techniques for efficient urban hive management, and record-keeping practices to monitor colony progress.

Frequency of Inspections and Key Indicators of Hive Health

- **How Often to Inspect**: Urban beekeepers should aim for a balance between monitoring their colonies closely and minimizing disturbances. During peak season (spring and summer), a bi-weekly inspection is recommended. In the off-season, monthly checks are sufficient.
- **What to Look For**: Key indicators of a healthy hive include active foraging behavior, consistent brood patterns, the presence of a queen or queen cells, and adequate stores of honey and pollen. Signs of distress or illness may include erratic brood patterns, a

noticeable decrease in population, the presence of pests or diseases, and aggressive behavior.

Tools and Techniques for Efficient Urban Hive Management

- **Essential Tools**: At a minimum, urban beekeepers should have a hive tool for opening the hive, a smoker to calm the bees, protective clothing to prevent stings, and a brush to gently move bees when necessary.
- **Techniques for Minimizing Disturbance**: Use smoke judiciously to calm the bees without overwhelming them. Open the hive gently and move slowly and deliberately to avoid agitating the bees. Whenever possible, schedule inspections during warm, sunny days when many bees are foraging and the hive is less crowded.

Record-Keeping Practices for Monitoring Colony Progress

- **Why Keep Records**: Keeping detailed records of each inspection helps track the colony's development over time, identify trends or issues early, and make informed decisions about interventions.
- **What to Record**: Note the date and weather conditions, hive behavior and mood, population size, brood pattern quality, honey and pollen stores, signs of pests or diseases, and any management actions taken.
- **How to Keep Records**: Options range from traditional beekeeping journals to digital apps designed for beekeeping records. Choose a method that fits your routine and preferences, ensuring it's easy to update and review.

By adhering to these guidelines for routine inspection and maintenance, urban beekeepers can ensure their hives remain healthy and productive. Regular monitoring and careful management are key to navigating the challenges of urban beekeeping, supporting not only the bees but also the broader ecosystem and community.

Seasonal Considerations in Urban Environments

Managing bee hives in urban settings requires a nuanced understanding of how seasonal changes impact bees, particularly in environments where traditional signs of the seasons may be less apparent. Urban beekeepers must be adept at recognizing and responding to the unique challenges and opportunities presented by each season, ensuring their colonies remain healthy and productive year-round. This section explores key strategies for preparing hives for extreme weather conditions, adjusting feeding and care to match urban foraging availability, and implementing winterizing techniques tailored to city environments.

Preparing Hives for Extreme Weather Conditions

- **Heat Waves and Urban Heat Islands**: Urban areas often experience higher temperatures due to the heat island effect. Providing adequate shade, ensuring proper ventilation, and offering supplemental water sources can help bees manage during hot spells.
- **Heavy Rains and Flooding**: Elevate hives off the ground to prevent water-logging during heavy rains, and consider windbreaks or barriers to protect hives from being battered by rain in exposed locations.
- **Cold Snaps**: Although urban areas may be warmer in winter, sudden cold snaps can occur. Insulate hives to protect against unexpected drops in temperature, taking care not to block hive entrances or ventilation.

Adjusting Feeding and Care Based on Urban Foraging Availability

- **Forage Scarcity**: Urban environments can experience periods of forage scarcity, particularly in early spring or late fall. Be prepared to supplement your bees' diet with sugar syrup or pollen patties during these times.
- **Seasonal Foraging Opportunities**: Take advantage of urban planting cycles by identifying local blooms in parks and gardens that

can provide forage for your bees. Adjust feeding practices based on the abundance of these resources.
- **Water Sources**: Ensure bees have access to clean water, especially in hot months. Urban beekeepers can set up water stations with pebbles or floating materials to provide bees with safe drinking points.

Winterizing Strategies Specific to Urban Settings

- **Insulation**: Urban beekeepers might need less insulation than rural beekeepers because of the urban heat island effect, but it's still crucial to provide some form of insulation to protect colonies from the cold.
- **Reduced Forage and Activity**: Recognize that bees will have reduced foraging opportunities and activity levels during colder months. Reduce hive inspections to minimize heat loss and stress on the colony.
- **Pest and Disease Management**: The end of the active season is a good time to treat for pests and diseases, ensuring your bees enter the colder months in good health. Urban environments may have different pest pressures than rural areas, so tailor your management practices accordingly.

Urban beekeeping demands flexibility and a proactive approach to seasonal changes. By understanding and anticipating the needs of your bees throughout the year, you can ensure that your urban hives not only survive but thrive, contributing to the biodiversity and beauty of the city landscape.

Pest and Disease Management

Common Urban Pests and Diseases to Watch For

Urban beekeeping introduces bees to a unique set of environmental factors and challenges, including specific pests and diseases that can threaten hive health. Common urban pests include Varroa mites, which can weaken bees and spread viruses, and small hive beetles, which thrive in warmer climates and can spoil honey stores. Diseases such as American Foulbrood (a bacterial infection that can destroy colonies) and Nosema (a fungal infection affecting bees' digestive systems) are also concerns in city environments. Urban beekeepers should be vigilant for signs of these pests and diseases, including irregular brood patterns, weakened or dead bees, and unusual hive smells or appearances.

Integrated Pest Management (IPM) Strategies for City Hives

Integrated Pest Management (IPM) is a sustainable approach to managing pests and diseases that minimize risks to bees, beekeepers, and the environment. IPM strategies for urban hives focus on prevention, monitoring, and control. Prevention involves maintaining strong, healthy colonies through proper nutrition and hive management practices.
 Monitoring requires regular hive inspections to detect early signs of pests or disease. Control measures should be applied judiciously, starting with the least invasive methods. Mechanical controls, such as drone comb removal for Varroa mite management, and cultural controls, like maintaining cleanliness around the hive, are preferred initial steps. Chemical controls, when necessary, should be selected for their low impact on bee health and honey quality.

Preventative Measures and Treatments for Urban Bee Colonies

Preventative measures are key to avoiding major pest and disease outbreaks in urban hives. Maintaining hygienic conditions within and around the hive can prevent the spread of pathogens. Regularly replacing old combs with new ones helps reduce disease build-up and pest populations. Beekeepers can also select bee varieties known for their resistance to certain pests and diseases. When treatment is necessary, it's important to choose options that are effective against the pest or disease while being safe for the bees, the beekeeper, and the urban environment. Natural and organic treatments, such as essential oils (e.g., thymol for Varroa mites) and microbial products (e.g., Bacillus thuringiensis for wax moth control), are often preferred in urban settings. Always follow local regulations and guidelines when applying treatments and consider the timing of treatments to minimize impact on bee activity and honey production.

Urban beekeepers play a critical role in managing pests and diseases, ensuring not only the health of their own hives but also the overall well-being of the urban bee population. By adopting IPM strategies and taking proactive preventative measures, beekeepers can maintain vibrant, productive colonies that contribute positively to the urban ecosystem.

Engaging with the Urban Community

Promoting Bee-Friendly Urban Spaces

Urban beekeeping extends beyond the confines of managing hives; it involves integrating beekeeping practices into the urban community in a manner that benefits both bees and people. A key aspect of this integration is promoting bee-friendly spaces within the city. By educating neighbors and community members about the benefits of beekeeping, initiating community projects to enhance urban foraging, and employing strategies to address concerns and conflicts, urban beekeepers can foster a supportive environment for their bees and contribute to the ecological health of their urban areas.

Educating Neighbors and Community Members about Beekeeping Benefits

- **Awareness Campaigns:** Organize informational sessions and workshops at local community centers, schools, and libraries to spread knowledge about the importance of bees in urban ecosystems, focusing on pollination, biodiversity, and the benefits of local honey production.
- **Open Hive Days:** Host open hive events, allowing people to see beekeeping up close and understand the complexity and beauty of bee colonies. This hands-on experience can dispel myths and

alleviate fears by educating the public on bee behavior and safety around hives.
- **Social Media and Online Platforms:** Utilize social media, blogs, and community forums to share stories, updates, and facts about urban beekeeping. Engaging content such as videos, photos, and beekeeping success stories can capture the interest of a wider audience.

Initiating Community Projects to Support Urban Foraging

- **Planting for Pollinators:** Collaborate with local authorities, schools, and community groups to create bee-friendly gardens and green spaces. Projects can include planting native flowers, setting up pollinator pathways, and converting unused land into forage-rich areas for bees.
- **Community Gardens:** Encourage and assist in establishing community gardens that incorporate pollinator-friendly plants. Providing advice and resources for garden planning can ensure these spaces offer valuable forage for urban bee populations throughout the seasons.
- **Partnerships with Local Businesses:** Work with local businesses to sponsor bee-friendly initiatives, such as adopting planters with pollinator-friendly plants or creating green roofs. Businesses can play a crucial role in expanding the forage available to urban bees.

Strategies for Resolving Conflicts and Concerns about Bees

- **Educational Outreach:** Address concerns directly by providing factual information about bees, particularly the low risk they pose when managed properly. Clarify the differences between honeybees and more aggressive species, such as wasps, to alleviate common fears.
- **Conflict Resolution Meetings:** Offer to meet with concerned parties, including neighbors and community groups, to discuss their worries and propose solutions. Being open, approachable, and willing to make adjustments can go a long way in resolving issues.

- **Creating Safe Spaces:** Implement hive management practices that minimize risks to neighbors, such as positioning hives away from high-traffic areas and using barriers that encourage bees to fly upwards over people's heads. Demonstrating a commitment to safety can help ease community concerns.

Engaging with the urban community in these ways means urban beekeepers can not only enhance the environment for their bees but also enrich the lives of city residents, fostering a greater appreciation for the vital role bees play in our world.

Collaboration and Support Networks

Urban beekeeping goes beyond just managing hives; it's about becoming part of a larger community effort to promote sustainability, biodiversity, and environmental awareness in city landscapes. Engaging with the urban community through collaboration and support networks can enrich your beekeeping experience, provide valuable resources, and foster a positive environment for bees and people alike. Here's how you can effectively connect and contribute to this vibrant community.

Joining Local Beekeeping Clubs and Online Forums

- **Networking and Knowledge Sharing:** Local beekeeping clubs offer a wealth of knowledge and experience. Members range from beginners to seasoned experts, providing a supportive environment for learning and sharing. Meetings and workshops can offer insights into urban beekeeping challenges and solutions.
- **Resources and Group Purchases:** Clubs often organize bulk purchases of beekeeping supplies, which can reduce costs. Access to shared resources like extractors or educational materials can also be a significant benefit.
- **Advocacy and Representation:** A collective voice can be more powerful in advocating for bee-friendly policies and practices within city councils or communities. Clubs play a crucial role in representing urban beekeepers' interests.

Partnering with Urban Agriculture and Sustainability Initiatives

- **Collaborative Projects:** Partnering with urban gardens, farms, and green spaces can provide foraging opportunities for your bees and help pollinate community and private gardens, enhancing local food production.
- **Educational Outreach:** Collaborations can lead to educational opportunities, such as workshops or school programs, promoting awareness of pollinators' roles in urban ecosystems.
- **Sustainability Efforts:** By aligning with sustainability initiatives, urban beekeepers can contribute to broader environmental goals, such as increasing urban green spaces and biodiversity.

Leveraging Community Resources for Educational and Support Purposes

- **Public Libraries and Community Centers:** These local institutions often offer space for meetings or educational events. They can be invaluable partners in hosting beekeeping workshops or talks, reaching a wider audience.
- **Grants and Funding:** Some communities offer grants for sustainability projects, including urban beekeeping. These funds can support hive installations in community gardens, schools, or other public spaces.
- **Social Media and Online Platforms:** using social media and online platforms can help spread the word about urban beekeeping, share experiences, and engage with a broader audience interested in sustainability and local food production.

If you actively engage with the urban community through collaboration and support networks, you can enhance your own experience while contributing positively to the environment and society. These connections not only provide practical benefits, such as shared resources and knowledge, but also foster a sense of community and collective action towards sustainable urban living.

Conclusion

As we conclude this exploration of hive management in limited urban spaces, it's clear that the constraints of city living offer a unique canvas for creativity and innovation in beekeeping. By thoughtfully selecting hive locations, utilizing space-efficient designs, and adhering to diligent maintenance routines, urban beekeepers can overcome the challenges posed by limited space. These strategies not only ensure the health and productivity of bee colonies but also enhance the urban environment, contributing to biodiversity and community well-being. Urban beekeeping becomes a testament to the resilience of both bees and their keepers, proving that with the right approaches, the bustling city landscape can indeed become a thriving home for bees. This chapter has aimed to equip urban beekeepers with the knowledge and tools necessary to navigate the complexities of city beekeeping, paving the way for successful and sustainable urban apiculture. As beekeepers integrate these practices, they join a growing community dedicated to fostering pollinator-friendly cities, highlighting the essential role bees play in our urban ecosystems and the importance of our continued stewardship.

Chapter 5: Health and Maintenance of Urban Bee Colonies

In the bustling heart of the city, where the rhythm of urban life intertwines with the natural world, maintaining the health and vitality of bee colonies presents a unique set of challenges and rewards. Chapter 5 delves into the essential practices of hive inspections, pest and disease management, and winter preparations tailored specifically for urban environments.

Through detailed guidance and practical advice, this chapter aims to equip urban beekeepers with the knowledge and tools necessary to ensure their hives not only survive but thrive amidst the concrete and crowds. From the nuances of detecting early signs of hive stress to implementing sustainable pest management strategies and preparing your bees for the colder months, we navigate the intricacies of urban bee health and maintenance. Embracing these practices means fostering resilient bee populations that contribute to the ecological health of our cities, ensuring a harmonious coexistence between urban dwellers and their winged pollinator counterparts.

Routine Hive Inspections

Frequency and Timing

Regular hive inspections are a cornerstone of successful beekeeping, especially in urban settings where environmental factors can vary significantly from one area to another. These inspections are crucial for assessing the health of the colony, spotting potential issues early, and making timely interventions to prevent disease, pest infestations, or resource shortages that could threaten the hive. However, it's equally important to balance the need for monitoring with the desire to minimize disturbance to the bees, ensuring they can go about their vital work with as little stress as possible.

The Importance of Regular Inspections

In the urban context, the close proximity of hives to human activity, coupled with the unique microclimates created by buildings and paved surfaces, can affect bee behavior and hive health. Regular inspections help beekeepers stay informed about their colonies' condition, enabling them to adjust management practices in response to urban environmental stressors. These check-ups allow for the monitoring of queen presence and performance, brood development, food storage levels, and any signs of disease or pests.

Best Times for Hive Inspections

Timing your inspections is key to minimizing disruption while maximizing the effectiveness of your observations. Ideally, inspections should be conducted during warm, calm days when most of the forager bees are out of the hive, typically between late morning and early afternoon. This reduces the number of bees in the hive during the inspection, lowering the stress on the colony and the risk of stinging incidents.

In urban areas, consider the specific climate variations and bee activity levels unique to your location. For instance, if your hive is in a shaded area that stays cooler longer, you might need to wait until midday when temperatures are more conducive to opening the hive. Similarly, if your hive is exposed to direct sunlight in a rooftop setting, early morning inspections might be preferable to avoid the peak heat of the day.

Seasonal Inspection Schedule

- **Spring:** This is a critical time for inspections, as colonies begin to grow with warmer weather. Weekly inspections can help ensure the queen is laying eggs effectively, and there is enough space for the colony to expand. It's also the time to check for any signs of swarming behavior and take preventive measures if necessary.
- **Summer:** Continue with bi-weekly inspections to monitor honey production and space requirements. This season demands vigilance

for pests and diseases, given the hive's high activity level. Ensure adequate ventilation and water availability during hotter periods.

- **Fall:** As the colony prepares for winter, reduce the inspection frequency to monthly. Check that the bees have sufficient stores for the winter and start to reduce the hive entrance to protect against pests.
- **Winter:** In colder climates, inspections should be minimal to avoid exposing the bees to cold air. A mid-winter check during a mild day can help assess food stores and overall hive health, but otherwise, disturbances should be kept to a bare minimum.

Adhering to this seasonal schedule helps maintain the balance between necessary oversight and the well-being of your urban bee colony. Regular, timely inspections are instrumental in identifying and addressing any issues before they become significant problems, ensuring the health and productivity of your bees amidst the urban landscape.

What to Look For

A thorough and observant approach to hive inspections is crucial for maintaining the health and productivity of your urban bee colonies. Knowing what to look for during these inspections can help you identify signs of a thriving hive as well as early warnings of potential issues. Here are the key indicators and signs to be aware of:

Key Indicators of a Healthy Hive

- **Brood Pattern**: A strong, healthy hive will have a consistent and compact brood pattern. Look for frames with densely packed brood cells, as this indicates a prolific queen. The presence of eggs, larvae, and capped brood should be visible, showing a continuous cycle of reproduction.
- **Queen Sighting**: Spotting the queen during an inspection is a positive sign, but not always necessary if you see evidence of her presence through fresh eggs. A healthy queen lays eggs in a

consistent pattern, and her ability to lay eggs is vital for the hive's growth and stability.

- **Population Density**: The strength of a colony is also reflected in its population density. A healthy hive will have a large number of bees covering the comb, actively working, feeding the brood, and storing nectar and pollen. Adequate population density is essential for completing all the tasks within the hive and for maintaining temperature control.
- **Honey Stores**: Ample honey stores indicate a productive hive. Inspect the frames to ensure there are sufficient honey and pollen reserves to feed the colony, particularly leading into the winter months. Well-stocked frames are a sign of a well-functioning hive that can support its population.

Signs of Stress or Disease

- **Irregular Brood Patterns**: Patchy or scattered brood patterns can mean issues within the hive, such as a failing or absent queen, disease, or nutritional deficiencies. Missing patches where eggs or larvae should be might also suggest problems with brood viability or queen health.
- **Presence of Pests**: Keep an eye out for pests such as Varroa mites, small hive beetles, or wax moths. Varroa mites, in particular, are a significant concern and can be spotted on bees or within brood cells. Pest management is crucial in urban beekeeping to prevent infestations that can weaken or destroy a colony.
- **Aggressive Behavior**: While bees can naturally become more defensive in response to certain threats, excessive aggression can be an indication of stress within the hive. Factors such as disease, queen issues, or environmental stressors can contribute to heightened defensive behavior.
- **Signs of Disease**: Look for symptoms of diseases such as American foulbrood (characterized by sunken, perforated cappings, and a foul odor) or chalkbrood (resulting in mummified larvae at the hive entrance). Early detection and management of diseases are critical to preventing their spread within and between urban hives.

Regularly conducting detailed inspections and understanding what to look for means urban beekeepers can take proactive steps to address any issues early on. This vigilance ensures not only the health and productivity of the hive but also its contribution to the urban ecosystem. Keeping detailed records of your observations during inspections can help track the hive's health over time and inform any necessary interventions to keep your urban bee colonies thriving.

Keeping a Beekeeping Journal

Maintaining a detailed beekeeping journal is an invaluable practice for urban beekeepers. It serves as a comprehensive record of hive health, bee behavior, and environmental changes over time. This practice not only helps in monitoring the immediate condition of your colonies but also provides insights for future management decisions and interventions.

Benefits of a Beekeeping Journal

Tracking Hive Health and Progress: A journal allows you to track the progress and health of your hives over time. By recording observations, you can identify patterns, such as growth in colony size, honey production rates, and brood rearing success, which are crucial for assessing the overall health and productivity of your bees.

Monitoring Bee Behavior: Documenting bee behavior, including foraging patterns, aggression levels, and swarming tendencies, helps in understanding the needs and stresses of your colony. Such records can be vital in preemptively addressing potential issues, ensuring a harmonious urban beekeeping experience.

Identifying Environmental Impact: Urban environments are dynamic, with varying factors like pollution, temperature fluctuations, and available forage affecting bee health. Keeping a log of these conditions alongside hive observations can help correlate environmental changes with bee health and behavior, guiding adjustments in management practices.

©Anthony Carter | www.beekeeping-101.com |part of Carman Online Content Publishing Ltd

Disease and Pest Management: Detailed records of any signs of disease, pest infestations, and the treatments applied enable you to manage hive health proactively. This historical data is invaluable for identifying what treatments have been effective and planning for preventative measures in future seasons.

Tips on Maintaining a Beekeeping Journal

What Information to Record

- **Date of Inspection:** Always note the date of each hive check.
- **Weather Conditions:** Record temperature, weather conditions, and any unusual environmental factors.
- **Hive Observations:** Note the presence of the queen, brood patterns, population size, behavior changes, signs of disease or pests, and honey stores.
- **Interventions:** Detail any actions taken during the inspection, such as feeding, treatments for pests or diseases, or hive modifications.
- **Floral Sources:** Keep track of blooming plants in the area, as this can affect foraging behavior and honey characteristics.

Using the Data for Long-term Hive Management

- **Review Regularly:** Periodically review your journal to identify trends or recurring issues. This can inform decisions on interventions, hive placements, and breeding choices.
- **Plan Ahead:** Use historical data to plan for seasonal management activities, such as supplemental feeding, swarm prevention strategies, and winter preparation.
- **Share Insights:** Your journal can be a valuable resource for the broader beekeeping community, especially for those facing similar urban beekeeping challenges. Sharing experiences and data can help improve urban beekeeping practices collectively.

A well-maintained beekeeping journal is more than just a log; it's a tool for informed decision-making and a diary of your journey through urban beekeeping. By systematically recording observations and actions, you create a rich source of knowledge that enhances the health and productivity of your colonies, contributing to the success and sustainability of urban beekeeping endeavors.

Pest and Disease Management in the City

Common Urban Bee Pests and Diseases

Urban beekeeping brings with it the responsibility of managing pests and diseases in environments where natural and human-made elements intersect. The health of bee colonies in the city is threatened by several pests and diseases, some of which are more prevalent or present unique challenges in urban settings. Understanding these threats is the first step towards effective management and ensuring the longevity and productivity of urban bee hives.

Varroa Mites

Varroa mites are perhaps the most significant and widespread pests affecting bee colonies worldwide, and urban hives are no exception. These parasitic mites attach themselves to bees, weakening them by feeding on their bodily fluids and spreading viruses. In the compact and closely-knit environments of urban beekeeping, Varroa mites can quickly spread from one colony to another, exacerbated by the high density of hives often found in city settings. Effective management includes regular monitoring using methods like the powdered sugar roll or alcohol wash, and when necessary, the application of approved miticides that are safe for use in populated areas.

American Foulbrood (AFB)

American Foulbrood is a bacterial disease that affects bee larvae, causing death and leading to the decay of brood within the hive. AFB spores are highly resistant to desiccation and can remain viable for years, posing a significant risk to nearby colonies. In urban environments, the close proximity of hives can facilitate the rapid spread of AFB, especially when beekeeping equipment is shared or bees rob from infected hives. Managing AFB in the city requires vigilance in inspecting brood frames, adherence to strict hygiene practices, and, in severe cases, the burning of infected hives and equipment to prevent the spread of the disease.

Small Hive Beetles (SHB)

Small Hive Beetles are opportunistic pests that thrive in warm climates and can cause significant damage to bee colonies by feeding on honey, pollen, and bee larvae. In urban areas, the microclimates created by buildings and pavement can provide ideal conditions for SHB populations to flourish. The beetles can also find refuge in the nooks and crannies of urban structures, making them difficult to control. Effective management strategies include maintaining strong and healthy colonies that can fend off SHB invasions, using traps within the hive, and ensuring proper hive hygiene to minimize attractants.

Unique Challenges in Urban Areas

The density of beekeeping operations in cities can amplify the challenges of pest and disease management. High bee population densities can lead to increased transmission rates of diseases and pests. Furthermore, the limited foraging options in some urban areas can stress colonies, making them more susceptible to diseases and pest infestations.

Urban beekeepers must also consider the impact of their pest and disease management choices on their neighbors and the environment. The use of chemicals to treat pests and diseases, for example, requires careful consideration and adherence to regulations to ensure the safety of humans, pets, and other wildlife in the area.

Collaboration and communication among urban beekeepers can play a vital role in managing these challenges. By sharing observations and strategies, beekeepers can create a coordinated defense against pests and diseases, enhancing the resilience of the urban beekeeping community as a whole.

Managing pests and diseases in urban bee colonies demands a proactive and informed approach. By understanding the specific threats and unique challenges of the urban environment, beekeepers can implement effective strategies to protect their hives and contribute to the health and vitality of the urban ecosystem.

Organic and Chemical Treatment Options

Urban beekeeping necessitates a balanced approach to managing pests and diseases, where the health of the bee colony and the urban environment are paramount. The choice between organic and chemical treatment options is critical, with each method offering its advantages and considerations. This section explores both approaches, guiding urban beekeepers in making informed decisions that promote sustainable practices.

Organic Methods

Mechanical Controls: Mechanical controls, such as drone comb removal and screened bottom boards, physically interrupt the lifecycle of pests like Varroa mites without the use of chemicals. These methods are effective and non-invasive, making them ideal for urban settings where environmental impact is a concern.

Natural Miticides: Natural miticides, including essential oils (such as thymol, eucalyptus, or mint oils) and formic acid, offer a way to control mite populations with substances that are less harmful to bees and more environmentally friendly. Their application must be carefully timed and dosed to minimize stress on the bees and avoid contamination of hive products.

Cultural Practices: Maintaining strong, healthy colonies through good hive management practices reduces vulnerability to pests and diseases. This includes ensuring adequate ventilation, proper nutrition, and hive hygiene. Urban beekeepers can also practice brood interruption techniques to control Varroa mite populations.

Chemical Treatments

Synthetic Acaricides: Synthetic acaricides, such as fluvalinate and coumaphos, are effective against Varroa mites but must be used judiciously to prevent mite resistance and residue buildup in wax and honey. Urban beekeepers should follow strict guidelines on dosages, treatment timing, and pre-harvest intervals to protect both bees and hive products.

Antibiotics for Bacterial Diseases: Antibiotics can be used to treat or prevent bacterial diseases like American foulbrood. However, their use is strictly regulated, and beekeepers must adhere to withdrawal times to ensure antibiotics do not contaminate honey. Moreover, the emphasis should be on using antibiotics as a last resort, with a focus on preventive measures and early detection.

Guidelines for Safe Application and Monitoring

Choosing the Right Treatment: Assess the specific needs of your colony and the severity of the pest or disease issue. Consider the lifecycle of the pest and the biology of your bees to choose the most effective and least disruptive treatment.

Application Timing and Dosage: Apply treatments according to the manufacturer's instructions or recommendations from reliable beekeeping resources. Timing is crucial to maximize efficacy and minimize impact on bee behavior and hive productivity, especially in urban areas where environmental concerns are heightened.

Monitoring and Assessment: After treatment, closely monitor the colony for signs of improvement or adverse reactions. Use hive inspection notes to track treatment efficacy and any side effects, adjusting your management practices based on observed outcomes.

Environmental Considerations: In urban settings, be especially mindful of the potential impact of treatments on non-target species and the broader environment. Choose treatments with the lowest risk of contamination to air, soil, and water, and communicate with neighbors about your beekeeping practices to foster understanding and cooperation.

Deciding between organic and chemical treatment options requires careful consideration of their impacts on bees, hive products, and the urban ecosystem. By prioritizing sustainable practices and informed decision-making, urban beekeepers can effectively manage pests and diseases, ensuring the health and longevity of their colonies in the city.

Preventive Measures for Urban Hive Health

Maintaining the health of bee colonies in urban environments requires proactive measures to prevent pests and diseases from taking hold. By adopting a holistic approach to hive management, urban beekeepers can create a strong foundation for their colonies, ensuring they are less susceptible to threats. This section outlines key preventive strategies, focusing on hygienic practices, regular inspections, and effective management of hive density.

Hygienic Practices

Equipment Sanitization: Regularly sanitize beekeeping tools and equipment to prevent the spread of pathogens. This includes cleaning smokers, hive tools, and extraction equipment with appropriate solutions after each use, especially when used on different hives.

Hive Component Rotation and Replacement: Rotate and replace hive components such as frames and foundation sheets periodically to control the buildup of pathogens and pests. Implementing a schedule for wax replacement can significantly reduce disease pressure within the hive.

Controlled Feeding: Ensure that feeding practices do not contribute to disease spread. Use clean, dedicated feeders and avoid exposing syrup or supplements to contamination. When feeding multiple hives, take care not to transfer feeders between hives without proper sanitation.

Regular Inspections

Consistent Monitoring: Conduct thorough hive inspections at regular intervals, with a keen eye for early signs of pest infestations or disease symptoms. Early detection is crucial for effective management and can often prevent wider colony impact.

Varroa Mite Monitoring: Implement regular monitoring for Varroa mites using methods such as sticky boards, alcohol washes, or sugar roll tests. Keeping mite levels under control is essential for maintaining colony health, especially in dense urban settings where infestations can quickly escalate.

Brood Health Checks: Pay close attention to the brood pattern during inspections. Healthy, consistent brood patterns are indicative of a strong queen and a healthy colony. Irregular patterns or missing brood can signal issues such as disease or queen problems.

Managing Hive Density

Appropriate Spacing: Maintain an appropriate number of hives for the available space and forage resources. Overcrowding can stress colonies, making them more susceptible to disease and leading to resource competition.

Disease Containment: In urban settings, where hives are often closer together than in rural areas, disease containment becomes critical. If a hive becomes diseased, take immediate action to treat the issue and prevent spread to other nearby hives. This may include quarantining the affected hive or implementing specific treatments.

Genetic Diversity: Promote genetic diversity within your apiary by sourcing queens from reputable breeders with a focus on disease resistance and temperament. Diverse genetics can enhance the colony's resilience to pests and diseases.

Integrating these preventive measures into your urban beekeeping practice means that you can create a healthier environment for your bees, mitigating the risk of pests and diseases. This proactive approach not only supports the longevity and productivity of your hives but also contributes to the broader health of the urban beekeeping community and the local ecosystem.

Preparing for Winter

Winterizing Your Hive in Urban Settings

As the vibrant colors of autumn fade into the crisp chill of winter, urban beekeepers face the critical task of preparing their hives for the colder months. Cities, with their unique microclimates, towering structures, and bustling activity, offer a different winter experience for bees compared to rural environments. Understanding how to effectively winterize your hive in such settings is essential for the survival and health of your bee colonies. This section provides a detailed look into the considerations and steps necessary to prepare your urban hives for winter.

Understanding Urban Microclimates

Urban areas can create microclimates that significantly affect the temperature and conditions around your hives. Buildings, asphalt, and concrete can absorb heat during the day and release it at night, sometimes offering a slightly warmer environment for your bees. However, these areas can also lead to erratic temperature fluctuations, which can be harmful to bees as they prepare for the winter. Recognizing the microclimate around your hive location will guide your winterization strategy, ensuring your bees are protected yet not overly insulated to the point of overheating on unexpectedly warm winter days.

Assessing Wind Exposure and Foraging Opportunities

In cities, tall buildings can create wind tunnels that significantly increase wind exposure to your hives. This can chill bees and reduce their ability to maintain the hive's temperature. Additionally, urban settings may offer limited foraging opportunities in late fall and early winter, affecting your bees' ability to stockpile necessary food reserves. Assessing both wind exposure and available foraging opportunities will inform how much supplemental feeding your bees might need and what windbreaks or sheltering strategies should be employed.

Step-by-Step Guide to Winterizing Urban Hives

1. **Insulation Techniques:**
   - Wrap hives with insulation materials that breathe, such as roofing felt or specially designed beehive wraps, to help maintain a stable internal temperature without trapping moisture inside.
   - Consider using rigid foam insulation boards on the top cover to reduce heat loss but ensure there's adequate ventilation to prevent condensation.

2. **Ventilation Adjustments:**
   - Ensure your hive has proper ventilation to allow moisture to escape. Moisture is a significant winter killer of bees, as it can lead to mold growth and chill the cluster.
   - Slightly prop open the top cover or use a moisture board with built-in ventilation to allow damp air to exit the hive while keeping the bees protected from direct wind.

3. **Hive Placement:**
   - If possible, adjust the hive's placement to take advantage of sunny spots that are shielded from prevailing winds. South-facing locations can offer more warmth during the day.
   - Consider relocating hives from rooftops to ground level or more sheltered areas if extreme wind or exposure is a concern. However, always weigh the stress of moving hives against the benefits.

4. **Reducing Hive Entrances:**
    *   Narrow the hive entrance to help bees defend against pests and reduce cold air influx. Use an entrance reducer or small pieces of wood to customize the entrance size.
    *   Ensure the entrance is clear of dead bees and debris to maintain proper air circulation.

5. **Supplemental Feeding:**
    *   Assess your hive's food stores in late fall. If stores are low, provide supplemental feeding with sugar syrup until temperatures drop below freezing, then switch to solid sugar feed or fondant.
    *   Place the feed close to the cluster to ensure bees have access even in cold weather.

6. **Water Access:**
    *   Bees need access to water, even in winter. Set up a water source protected from freezing, such as a container with floating wood or foam pieces that bees can land on, near your hive.

By attentively preparing your urban hives for winter, considering the unique challenges of city environments, you can significantly increase your bees' chances of surviving the cold months. This preparation enables them to emerge strong and healthy for the next season, continuing their vital role in urban pollination and biodiversity.

Feeding and Care During Colder Months

As the vibrant buzz of summer fades into the quiet chill of winter, the focus for urban beekeepers shifts towards ensuring their colonies have sufficient resources to make it through the colder months. In urban settings, where natural forage can be scarce even before the onset of winter, supplemental feeding becomes crucial. This section explores effective feeding strategies and the importance of water access during winter, ensuring your bees remain healthy and well-nourished until spring.

Supplemental Feeding Strategies

1. When to Start Feeding
- Begin supplemental feeding when you notice a decrease in natural forage availability, typically in late summer or early fall before temperatures drop significantly.
- Monitor honey stores in your hives; if they're insufficient for winter (bees need approximately 30-60 pounds of honey), it's time to supplement.

2. Feeding Sugar Syrup
- In early fall, feed a thicker syrup (2 parts sugar to 1 part water) to mimic the consistency of honey, providing energy for the bees to generate warmth.
- Use feeders that attach directly to the hive to minimize disturbance and ensure easy access for the bees.

3. Transitioning to Fondant or Candy Boards
- As temperatures continue to drop, liquid feedings become less practical. Transition to solid feeding options like fondant or candy boards, which don't freeze and are easy for bees to consume during cold weather.
- Place fondant directly above the cluster or on top of the frames where bees cluster in winter, ensuring they have direct access without having to venture far in cold conditions.

Water Access During Winter

1. The Importance of Water
- Even in winter, bees need water to dilute stored honey for consumption and to maintain humidity levels within the hive.
- Providing a water source is crucial, especially in urban areas where natural sources may freeze or be scarce.

2. Preventing Freezing
- Use shallow containers with floating materials such as small sticks or corks to prevent bees from drowning and to insulate the water.

- Place water sources in sunny spots to take advantage of solar warmth, or use heated water dishes specifically designed for poultry, ensuring they are safe and accessible for bees.

3. **Innovative Urban Solutions**
   - Consider insulating water sources with natural materials or using solar-powered water heaters to keep water from freezing.
   - Collaborate with neighbors or community gardens to identify and maintain shared water sources for urban wildlife, including bees.

Implementing these feeding and water provision strategies means that urban beekeepers can significantly improve their colonies' chances of surviving the winter. Supplemental feeding with sugar syrup and fondant provides the necessary calories for warmth and energy, while ensuring access to water aids in food digestion and overall hive health. As each urban environment presents its own challenges, beekeepers may need to adapt these strategies to fit their specific circumstances. The goal is to enter spring with strong, healthy colonies ready to take advantage of the first blooms.

Monitoring Hive Health in Winter

Winter poses a significant challenge for beekeepers, particularly in urban settings where the environment can vary dramatically from one block to the next. Monitoring hive health during these colder months is crucial, yet it must be done with care to avoid exposing bees to harmful cold stress. This section provides guidance on how to safely check on your bees during winter and outlines the signs of a healthy winter colony as well as the red flags that may indicate problems requiring intervention.

How to Safely Check on Your Bees in Winter

Minimize Hive Openings: In winter, it's vital to keep the hive as undisturbed as possible. Opening the hive should be avoided unless absolutely necessary, as it can let in cold air and chill the bees. If you must open the hive, choose a mild, sunny day when the temperature is at least above 50°F (10°C), and work quickly to minimize heat loss.

Use External Inspection Methods: You can learn a lot about the health of your hive through external observations. Check the hive entrance for dead bees and clear them away to maintain ventilation. Observe the entrance on warmer days for bee activity, indicating that the colony is still active. Listening at the hive's side with a stethoscope or a simple ear-against-the-hive method can also reveal the comforting hum of a living, working colony.

Weight Checks: Lifting the back of the hive slightly can give you an indication of the honey stores remaining. A heavy hive suggests that there are still ample stores, while a light hive might mean that additional feeding is necessary.

Signs of a Healthy Winter Colony

Consistent Humming Sound: A healthy winter colony will produce a low, steady humming sound, indicating that bees are clustering to keep warm and are actively regulating the temperature of the hive.

Limited Entrance Activity: On warmer winter days, seeing bees venturing out for cleansing flights is a good sign. It shows the colony is alive and well, with bees taking the opportunity to eliminate waste outside the hive.

Evidence of Food Consumption: Signs that bees are consuming their stored honey and pollen, visible during brief and necessary inspections, are indicative of a functioning colony. Bees naturally move up through the hive in winter, consuming the stores they've accumulated above them.

Red Flags Indicating Problems

Silence or Weak Buzzing: A lack of sound or a very faint buzzing from within the hive might indicate a problem, such as a dead or dying colony.

No Activity on Warm Days: If there's an unseasonably warm day and no bees are seen exiting the hive for cleansing flights, this could be a sign of trouble.

Foul Odors: A bad smell emanating from the hive could mean disease or decay inside, necessitating a closer inspection.

Excessive Dead Bees at the Entrance: While some die-off is normal, a large number of dead bees at the hive entrance, especially if blocking the entrance, can indicate a problem within the hive.

Monitoring your bees during winter requires a balance between vigilance and minimal interference. By employing these methods, urban beekeepers can ensure their colonies remain healthy through the winter, ready to emerge in spring and contribute to the urban ecosystem once more. Always prioritize the bees' welfare in your winter checks, intervening only when necessary to support the hive's health and survival.

Conclusion

Maintaining the health and vitality of urban bee colonies requires diligent care, regular inspections, and a proactive approach to pest and disease management. Urban beekeepers face unique challenges, from navigating the constraints of limited space to addressing the specific needs of bees in a city environment. However, by adhering to the guidelines outlined in this chapter, including conducting thorough hive inspections, employing sustainable pest management strategies, and preparing hives for the winter months, beekeepers can ensure their colonies not only survive but thrive in urban settings.

Embracing these practices fosters healthy bee populations, which in turn enhances urban biodiversity and supports the broader ecosystem. As urban beekeepers, we have the opportunity to make a significant positive impact on our local environments, demonstrating that even in the heart of the city, nature can flourish with care, knowledge, and community cooperation.

Chapter 6: Urban Foraging for Bees

In the heart of the concrete jungle, amidst towering skyscrapers and bustling streets, lies an oasis of biodiversity often overlooked: urban forage for bees. Urban environments, contrary to popular belief, can teem with a diverse range of foraging opportunities for our pollinating friends. This chapter unveils the hidden potential of city landscapes as vital sources of nectar and pollen, essential for the health and productivity of urban bee colonies.

We will explore how to identify, enhance, and create foraging opportunities within the urban maze, transforming the way we think about and interact with our urban ecosystems. From mapping out forage sources to collaborating with community gardens and initiating pollinator-friendly projects, this section is a comprehensive guide designed to equip urban beekeepers with the knowledge and tools necessary to support their hives through the art and science of urban foraging. Join us as we delve into the world of urban bee foraging, where every rooftop, balcony, and garden hold the potential to become a haven for bees, contributing to a more sustainable and bee-friendly city environment.

Understanding Urban Forage Sources

Mapping Urban Forage

In the quest to support urban bee populations, the first step for any beekeeper is to understand the lay of the land. Urban environments are not barren wastelands but are instead dotted with rich sources of forage for bees. These sources include public parks, private gardens, roadside greenery, and increasingly popular green roofs. Mapping these forage areas is crucial for effective hive placement and developing strategic foraging paths for your bees. Here's how you can get started with mapping urban forage for your bees:

©Anthony Carter | www.beekeeping-101.com | part of Carman Online Content Publishing Ltd

Identify Potential Forage Sources: Begin by identifying potential forage sources within flying distance of your proposed hive location. Bees typically forage within a 3 to 5 km radius, so consider this range as your mapping boundary. Look for areas with floral diversity, as bees thrive on a varied diet. Parks, gardens, and even cemeteries can be excellent sources of nectar and pollen.

Utilize Online Tools and Resources: Leverage the power of online tools such as Google Maps and local botanical garden databases to identify green spaces in your city. Some cities also have dedicated apps or websites mapping out green spaces and public gardens, which can be invaluable in your search.

Conduct Field Surveys: While online tools provide a good starting point, nothing beats the accuracy of a personal survey. Take walks or bike rides around your neighborhood to spot flowering plants, trees, and shrubs. Note the types of vegetation and their blooming periods, as this information will help you plan for year-round forage availability.

Engage with Local Gardening Communities: Local gardening clubs and community garden associations can be treasure troves of information on plant species that thrive in your area. These communities often engage in planting bee-friendly flora and can provide insights into local forage sources you may have overlooked.

Document Forage Sources: As you identify potential forage areas, document them using a map or a digital app. Mark locations with significant floral diversity and note any seasonal variations in plant life. This map will become an essential tool in planning your hives' placements and foraging strategies.

Consider Planting Seasons: Understanding the planting and blooming seasons of your local flora is crucial. Aim to ensure that your bees have a consistent source of forage throughout their active months. This may involve advocating for the planting of late-blooming species in public spaces or incorporating these into your own garden.

©Anthony Carter | www.beekeeping-101.com | part of Carman Online Content Publishing Ltd

Collaborate with Urban Planners and Landscapers: Establishing contact with city planners and landscapers can open up opportunities to influence the planting of bee-friendly flora in public spaces. Many urban areas are adopting pollinator-friendly policies, and beekeepers can play a pivotal role in these initiatives by providing expertise and recommendations.

Mapping urban forage is an ongoing process, reflecting the dynamic nature of urban ecosystems and landscaping trends. By understanding and engaging with the urban landscape, beekeepers can significantly enhance the foraging options available to their bees, contributing to healthier colonies and a richer urban biodiversity. This proactive approach not only benefits the bees but also enriches the urban environment, creating a symbiotic relationship between urban dwellers and nature.

Common Urban Forage Plants

Urban environments, often perceived as desolate spaces for wildlife, surprisingly harbor a rich diversity of plant life that can support bee populations. Understanding which plants serve as valuable forage sources for bees is crucial for urban beekeepers. This section provides a detailed list of common urban forage plants, offering insights into their recognition and blooming cycles, enabling beekeepers to ensure their bees have access to essential resources throughout the year.

Trees

- **Linden (*Tilia spp.*)**: Linden trees are a favorite among bees, with their fragrant blossoms offering abundant nectar. They typically bloom in early to mid-summer, providing a significant forage source during these months.
- **Maple (*Acer spp.*)**: Early in the spring, maple trees are among the first to provide pollen and nectar, crucial for bees coming out of winter dormancy. Look for their distinctive flowers before the leaves fully emerge.
- **Cherry (*Prunus spp.*)**: Cherry trees, with their early spring blossoms, offer a critical nectar source when few other plants are

blooming. Their flowers are not only a boon for bees but also a visual treat for city dwellers.

Shrubs

- **Butterfly Bush (*Buddleja davidii*)**: This fast-growing shrub blooms from summer to fall, attracting bees with its nectar-rich flowers. Its various colors and continuous blooming make it an excellent choice for urban gardens.
- **Lavender (*Lavandula spp.*)**: Lavender is well-loved for its aroma and purple blooms. Thriving in sunny spots, it's a go-to for urban beekeepers, blooming in late spring to early summer.
- **Rosemary (*Rosmarinus officinalis*)**: With its preference for warm, sunny locations, rosemary can bloom almost year-round in milder urban climates, providing a steady source of nectar and pollen.

Flowers

- **Sunflowers (*Helianthus annuus*)**: Sunflowers are not just visually striking; their large blooms are excellent nectar and pollen sources in late summer and early fall.
- **Zinnias (*Zinnia elegans*)**: Offering a burst of color from summer to fall, zinnias are easy to grow and highly attractive to bees. They're ideal for adding vibrancy and forage to any urban space.
- **Clover (*Trifolium spp.*)**: Often found in lawns and parks, clover is a significant nectar source. While considered a weed by some, its value for bees is undeniable, especially during its peak blooming in spring and summer.

Herbs

- **Basil (*Ocimum basilicum*)**: Basil's flowers, if allowed to bloom, provide nectar and pollen in the summer. It's a dual-purpose plant, offering culinary uses and supporting urban bees.
- **Mint (*Mentha spp.*)**: Mint blooms in mid to late summer, attracting bees with its tiny, abundant flowers. It's adaptable to various urban settings but can be invasive, so container planting is recommended.

©Anthony Carter | www.beekeeping-101.com | part of Carman Online Content Publishing Ltd

- **Blooming Cycles**: Familiarize yourself with the blooming cycles of these plants to ensure your bees have continuous forage. Planting a variety of species that bloom at different times can provide bees with resources from early spring through late fall.
- **Plant Identification**: Learn to identify these plants by their distinctive leaves, flowers, and growth habits. This knowledge will help you spot potential forage sources in your urban environment and choose the best plants for your own bee garden.
- **Forage Enhancement**: Encourage the planting of bee-friendly trees, shrubs, and flowers in community gardens, parks, and other public spaces. Taking part in local urban greening projects can significantly enhance forage availability for bees.

If you incorporate these common urban forage plants into your beekeeping practice, either by identifying existing sources or planting new ones, you can significantly improve the health and productivity of your urban bee colonies.

Creating an Urban Bee Garden

Selecting Plants for Pollinators

Creating an urban bee garden is a rewarding endeavor that not only supports the local bee population but also enhances the beauty and biodiversity of urban spaces. The key to a successful bee garden lies in the selection of plants that provide a continuous source of nectar and pollen throughout the bee active seasons. This section will guide you through choosing the right plants to nourish your urban pollinators, ensuring they have access to the resources they need to thrive.

Understanding Nectar and Pollen Sources: Bees require nectar for energy and pollen for protein. When selecting plants for your bee garden, aim for a variety that offers both. Some plants are rich in nectar, while others are valued for their high pollen content. A balanced mix ensures bees receive a comprehensive diet.

Seasonal Blooming: One of the most important considerations is to ensure that your garden has plants blooming from early spring through late fall. This continuous bloom provides bees with a steady food source throughout their active months. Early spring flowers help bees build up strength after winter, summer blooms sustain them during the peak of their activity, and late-blooming plants prepare them for the upcoming winter.

Plant Selection for Urban Spaces: Urban spaces often come with limitations, such as small areas or container-only gardening. However, many plants that are beneficial to bees can thrive in containers or small spaces. Here is a guide to help you select the right plants:

- **Spring:** Crocus, hyacinth, borage, and early blooming fruit trees like cherry and apple provide the first nectar and pollen sources after winter.
- **Summer:** Lavender, thyme, oregano, and bee balm are excellent mid-season providers, offering abundant nectar and pollen.
- **Fall:** Sedum, goldenrod, and asters are late bloomers that offer vital support to bees preparing for winter.

Container Gardening for Pollinators: Even with no ground space, container gardening can be a boon for urban bees. Select pots of various sizes to accommodate different root depths and choose plants that are well-suited for container life. Herbs, such as basil, chives, and mint, are not only great for bees, but can also be used in your kitchen.

Plant Diversity: Diversity is crucial in a bee garden. Aim to plant native species whenever possible, as these are often best suited to the local bee population. Exotic plants can also be beneficial, provided they are not invasive or harmful to local ecosystems. A diverse plant selection ensures a wider range of nutritional offerings for bees and can attract different bee species and other pollinators.

©Anthony Carter | www.beekeeping-101.com |part of Carman Online Content Publishing Ltd

Water Sources: Besides plants, bees need access to clean water. A shallow bird bath with stones for bees to land on or a dripping water feature can provide a much-needed drinking spot for your pollinating visitors.

Carefully selecting plants that cater to the needs of bees throughout the year means you can create a vibrant and productive urban bee garden in even the smallest of spaces. This not only aids in the survival of urban bee populations but also contributes to the overall health of our urban environments, bringing a touch of nature's bounty into the heart of the city.

Garden Design for Bees

Designing a garden that attracts bees is an art that marries aesthetics with functionality, transforming urban spaces into thriving sanctuaries for bees. A well-planned bee garden not only supports local bee populations but also enhances the beauty and biodiversity of urban environments. Here, we delve into the essential components of garden design that cater specifically to the needs of bees, focusing on plant diversity, color selection, layout optimization, and the provision of water sources and shelter.

Plant Diversity

A diverse selection of plants is crucial for a bee-friendly garden. Diversity ensures a steady supply of nectar and pollen throughout the growing season, catering to the varied tastes and needs of different bee species. Incorporate a mix of native plants, herbs, vegetables, and ornamentals that bloom at different times to provide continuous forage. Plants like lavender, rosemary, thyme, and sage offer rich nectar sources, while sunflowers, asters, and zinnias attract bees with their pollen.

Color Attraction

Bees are particularly drawn to certain colors, with blue, purple, white, and yellow flowers being the most attractive. Incorporating these colors into your garden design can significantly increase its allure for bees. Cluster plants of similar colors together to create a visual beacon for bees flying overhead. However, remember that bees perceive colors differently than humans, so including a variety of hues will cater to a broader range of bee species.

Garden Layout

The layout of your bee garden should facilitate easy access to food sources with minimal exposure to predators. Consider planting in clusters or drifts to create dense pockets of forage, which is more appealing to bees than scattered individual plants. Incorporate different heights and structures, such as trellises or raised beds, to add dimension and make the garden more navigable for bees. Paths between plantings can also enhance accessibility for both bees and gardeners.

Water Sources

Bees need water for drinking and cooling their hives, making water sources a critical component of a bee garden. Shallow water features, such as birdbaths with stones or floating wood for bees to land on, can provide safe drinking spots. Alternatively, a dripping faucet or a water garden can also attract bees. Ensure the water is clean and replenished regularly to maintain its appeal.

Shelter and Habitat

Providing shelter is essential for protecting bees from predators and harsh weather conditions. Dense vegetation, bee hotels, or even a pile of natural materials can offer refuge for solitary bees. For honeybees, consider the placement of hives within the garden, ensuring they are protected from direct sunlight and strong winds. Native plants and grasses can also offer nesting sites for ground-nesting bees, enhancing the habitat diversity of your garden.

Creating an urban bee garden is a rewarding endeavor that benefits both bees and humans. By considering plant diversity, color, layout, water sources, and shelter, urban beekeepers and gardeners can develop spaces that support pollinator health and contribute to the ecological well-being of urban areas. A thoughtfully designed bee garden becomes a living mosaic of colors, scents, and textures, inviting a closer connection with nature in the urban landscape.

Maintaining Your Bee Garden

Creating an urban bee garden is a significant step towards supporting urban bees, but the journey doesn't end with planting. To ensure your garden remains a thriving sanctuary for pollinators, ongoing maintenance is crucial. Here, we explore best practices for sustaining a healthy bee garden, focusing on organic pest control and soil health, integral components of an eco-friendly urban oasis.

Organic Pest Control

Pesticides and insecticides, while effective against unwanted pests, can be harmful to bees and other beneficial insects. Adopting organic pest control methods not only protects the pollinators but also maintains the ecological balance in your garden.

- **Physical Barriers**: Utilize physical barriers such as netting or floating row covers to protect plants from pests without harming bees. These barriers can be particularly effective against larger pests while allowing bees to access flowers during their foraging hours.
- **Beneficial Insects**: Encourage or introduce beneficial insects like ladybugs, lacewings, and predatory mites that naturally control pest populations. A biodiverse garden attracts these natural allies, creating a self-regulating ecosystem.
- **Companion Planting**: Planting certain herbs and flowers can naturally repel pests. For example, marigolds deter nematodes and chives repel aphids. Companion planting also enhances biodiversity, providing a range of foraging options for bees.
- **Homemade and Natural Pesticides**: When necessary, opt for homemade or natural pesticides such as neem oil, soap spray, or chili pepper spray. These remedies offer a less harmful alternative

to chemical pesticides, minimizing the risk to bees. Always apply them in the evening or early morning when bees are less active.

Soil Health

Healthy soil is the foundation of any garden, and a bee garden is no exception. Nutrient-rich, well-drained soil supports a diverse range of plants that bees love, ensuring your garden is as nourishing as it is beautiful.

- **Organic Matter**: Regularly enrich your soil with organic matter such as compost, leaf mold, or well-rotted manure. This not only improves soil fertility but also enhances its water-retention capabilities, ensuring plants remain hydrated and healthy.
- **Mulching**: Apply a layer of organic mulch around your plants to conserve moisture, suppress weeds, and gradually improve soil quality as it decomposes. Mulch also provides a habitat for many ground-dwelling beneficial insects.
- **No-Till Gardening**: Minimize soil disturbance by adopting a no-till or minimal tillage approach. This technique preserves soil structure, reduces erosion, and helps maintain a healthy community of soil organisms that benefit plant growth and health.
- **Watering Practices**: Efficient watering practices are essential, especially in urban settings where water may be scarce. Drip irrigation or soaker hoses deliver water directly to the plant roots, reducing evaporation and minimizing water waste. Early morning watering reduces fungal diseases and ensures plants are well-hydrated throughout the day.

If you implement these practices, you can ensure your urban bee garden is not only a vibrant and productive space for bees but also a model of sustainable urban gardening. A well-maintained bee garden becomes a cornerstone of urban ecology, supporting pollinators, enhancing biodiversity, and contributing to the health of our urban environments.

Collaborating with Urban Green Spaces

Engaging with Community Gardens and Parks

Urban green spaces, such as community gardens and city parks, are invaluable assets in the quest to support and enhance bee populations in city environments. These areas provide essential foraging grounds for bees, offering a variety of flowering plants that supply nectar and pollen throughout the growing season. Collaborating with these spaces not only expands the foraging landscape for urban bees, but also fosters a sense of community and shared responsibility towards our environment. Here's how urban beekeepers can effectively engage with community gardens and parks to promote pollinator-friendly practices:

Understanding the Importance of Community Spaces

- **Recognizing Value**: Begin by acknowledging the crucial role that community gardens and parks play in urban ecology. These spaces serve as green corridors that support a wide range of pollinators, including bees, by providing them with habitat and food resources.
- **Educational Opportunities**: Use these engagements as opportunities to educate others about the importance of bees in urban settings. Highlight how bees contribute to the health of gardens and parks through pollination, which in turn benefits the entire community by enhancing plant diversity and productivity.

Building Relationships

- **Connect with Managers and Volunteers**: Identify and reach out to individuals who manage or volunteer at community gardens and parks. Establishing a rapport with these key stakeholders is the first step toward collaborative efforts.
- **Offer Your Expertise**: As a beekeeper, you bring valuable knowledge about pollinators that can benefit the management of these green

spaces. Offer to share your insights through workshops, informational sessions, or informal discussions.

Advocating for Pollinator-Friendly Plantings

- **Suggest Plant Varieties**: Recommend a list of pollinator-friendly plants that thrive in your local climate and urban conditions. Emphasize plants that provide blooms throughout the year to ensure a consistent food source for bees.
- **Promote Organic Practices**: Encourage the use of organic gardening practices to protect pollinators from harmful pesticides. Discuss natural pest control methods and the importance of maintaining chemical-free spaces for bees and other wildlife.

Collaborative Projects and Initiatives

- **Pollinator Gardens**: Propose the creation of dedicated pollinator gardens within community spaces. These gardens can serve as educational tools and beautiful attractions that raise awareness about pollinators.
- **Habitat Enhancement**: Work together on projects that enhance habitat for bees, such as installing bee hotels, creating water sources, and planting native wildflowers.
- **Community Events**: Organize or take part in events that promote pollinator conservation, such as plant sales, beekeeping demonstrations, and pollinator awareness campaigns.

Navigating Challenges

- **Address Concerns**: Be prepared to address common concerns about bees, such as safety and allergies. Provide factual information and strategies to coexist safely with bees in community spaces.
- **Seek Common Ground**: Find a balance between the needs and interests of the community and the goal of supporting urban bees. Compromise and flexibility are key to successful collaboration.

Measuring Success

- **Monitor Impact**: Keep track of the changes in plant diversity and bee activity in the areas where you've been involved. This data can be valuable in demonstrating the positive impact of your efforts.
- **Celebrate Achievements**: Share successes with the community through social media, local news outlets, and community meetings. Highlighting achievements can inspire further action and support for pollinator-friendly initiatives.

Engaging with community gardens and parks means that urban beekeepers can play a pivotal role in enhancing the urban landscape for bees. These collaborations not only improve foraging opportunities for bees, but also strengthen community bonds and raise awareness about the importance of pollinators in maintaining healthy, vibrant urban ecosystems.

Creating Pollinator Pathways

In the quest to support urban bee populations, the concept of pollinator pathways has emerged as a transformative approach to enhancing urban foraging landscapes. Pollinator pathways are networks of green spaces that are intentionally connected to provide bees, butterflies, and other pollinators with continuous habitats rich in nectar and pollen sources. These pathways not only facilitate easier movement and foraging for pollinators across urban areas, but also contribute to the ecological health and biodiversity of cities.

Understanding Pollinator Pathways

Pollinator pathways are created by linking small patches of pollinator-friendly environments such as gardens, parks, green roofs, and other green spaces. These links form a "corridor" that pollinators can navigate, helping them to find food and shelter more efficiently in urban settings. The aim is to mitigate the effects of habitat fragmentation, a common issue in cities where natural landscapes are interrupted by buildings and roads, creating barriers for pollinators.

Urban Beekeepers as Catalysts for Change

Urban beekeepers are uniquely positioned to advocate for and contribute to the development of pollinator pathways. By collaborating with local governments, community groups, and environmental organizations, beekeepers can help to identify potential sites for pollinator-friendly plantings and work towards connecting these areas. Beekeepers can also transform their own gardens or beekeeping sites into nodes within the pollinator pathway, serving as examples of how private and public spaces can be used effectively for this purpose.

Steps to Creating Pollinator Pathways

- **Mapping Potential Pathways**: Begin by identifying existing green spaces in your urban area that can serve as starting points or nodes in the pathway. Utilize maps and local environmental resources to chart a course that links these spaces together.
- **Engagement and Collaboration**: Reach out to local authorities, community garden groups, and environmental organizations to discuss the concept of pollinator pathways. Collaboration is key to securing support and resources for the project.
- **Choosing the Right Plants**: Selecting native plants that provide nectar and pollen throughout the growing season is crucial. Diversity in plant selection ensures a wide range of pollinators can benefit.
- **Educating the Community**: Raising awareness about the importance of pollinator pathways is essential. Workshops, talks, and informational materials can help to engage the community and encourage participation in the project.
- **Monitoring and Maintenance**: Once established, pollinator pathways require ongoing care. Monitoring the health of the plants and the activity of pollinators can provide valuable feedback for the effectiveness of the pathway.

Benefits of Pollinator Pathways

The creation of pollinator pathways has many benefits for urban environments. Beyond supporting pollinator populations, these green corridors can improve the aesthetic value of cities, enhance air quality, and provide educational opportunities for residents about the importance of biodiversity and conservation. For urban beekeepers, these pathways ensure their hives have access to a consistent and diverse range of forage options, crucial for the health and productivity of their bees.

Pollinator pathways represent a powerful strategy for enhancing urban ecology and supporting bee populations. Urban beekeepers, with their deep understanding of pollinator needs and challenges, are at the forefront of this movement. By initiating and participating in the creation of these pathways, beekeepers can make a significant impact on the sustainability and biodiversity of urban landscapes, paving the way for a more pollinator-friendly future.

Partnerships with Municipalities and Businesses

In the quest to expand urban foraging opportunities for bees, establishing partnerships with local governments and businesses emerges as a critical strategy. These collaborations can lead to impactful initiatives that not only benefit bees, but also enhance community well-being and environmental health. Here, we explore various approaches urban beekeepers can take to foster these partnerships, highlighting the mutual benefits and offering guidance on navigating these collaborative efforts.

Engaging with Local Government

Local governments play a pivotal role in urban planning and green space management, making them essential allies in the promotion of bee-friendly environments. Urban beekeepers can engage with municipal authorities through:

- **Advocacy for Bee-Friendly Policies**: Lobby for the integration of pollinator-friendly practices in urban landscaping and development plans. This includes advocating for the use of native plants in public parks, green roofs on municipal buildings, and the establishment of pollinator corridors across the city.
- **Participating in Urban Greening Projects**: Volunteer to consult on or take part in city-led greening projects, offering expertise on plant selection and hive management to ensure these initiatives are beneficial for local bee populations.
- **Grant and Funding Opportunities**: Explore grants and funding provided by local governments for sustainability projects. Propose initiatives that align with urban beekeeping and foraging enhancement, such as creating pollinator gardens in community spaces or educational programs about the importance of bees in urban ecosystems.

Forming Partnerships with Businesses

Businesses, from small local shops to large corporations, can significantly contribute to creating urban foraging opportunities. Partnerships can be formed through:

- **Sponsoring Bee-Friendly Plantings**: Encourage businesses to sponsor the planting of bee-friendly flora around their premises or in nearby public spaces. This not only supports urban foraging but can also enhance the aesthetic appeal and environmental quality of the area, reflecting positively on the business.
- **Adopting Green Space Initiatives**: Collaborate with businesses to adopt unused or underutilized land for the creation of pollinator gardens. These spaces can serve as valuable foraging sites for bees and educational resources for the community, promoting corporate social responsibility.
- **Employee Engagement Programs**: Work with businesses to develop employee engagement programs focused on sustainability and bee conservation. Activities could include workshops on beekeeping, planting days, or adopting a hive, fostering a connection between the workforce and the local environment.

Building Mutual Benefits

The key to successful partnerships with municipalities and businesses lies in highlighting the mutual benefits. For urban areas, increased forage for bees supports biodiversity, enhances green spaces, and contributes to the well-being of the community. For businesses, participating in these initiatives can improve their public image, engage employees in meaningful sustainability efforts, and contribute to their environmental goals.

Navigating Collaborative Efforts

When approaching potential partners, be prepared with a clear proposal outlining the benefits, requirements, and expected outcomes of the initiative. Demonstrating the success of similar projects, either locally or in other cities, can help build your case. Maintaining open communication, setting realistic goals, and ensuring that all parties are aligned in their objectives are crucial for the success and sustainability of these partnerships.

Through strategic collaboration with local governments and businesses, urban beekeepers can play a pivotal role in transforming cities into thriving ecosystems for bees. These partnerships not only expand foraging opportunities but also foster a greater sense of community and environmental stewardship among urban dwellers, paving the way for a more sustainable and bee-friendly future.

Urban Forage Enhancement Projects

Seed Bombing and Guerrilla Gardening

In the quest to expand urban foraging options for bees, innovative and proactive methods are essential. Among these, seed bombing and guerrilla gardening stand out as creative and impactful approaches to greening our cities. These grassroots tactics not only enhance the urban landscape for

©Anthony Carter | www.beekeeping-101.com | part of Carman Online Content Publishing Ltd

pollinators but also foster a sense of community and environmental stewardship among city dwellers.

Seed Bombing: Aerial Reforestation for Urban Bees

Seed bombing, or aerial reforestation, is a technique that involves throwing or dropping balls made of clay, compost, and seeds into barren or underutilized urban areas. This method allows for the rapid planting of pollinator-friendly vegetation with minimal disturbance to the land.

- **Making Seed Bombs**: Crafting seed bombs is simple and can be an engaging community activity. The basic ingredients include natural clay, compost, water, and seeds of native flowers known for their high nectar and pollen content. Mix these components until you achieve a pliable consistency, then roll the mixture into small balls. Allow them to dry for 24-48 hours before launching your green grenades into targeted areas.
- **Choosing the Right Seeds**: Selecting seeds for your seed bombs is crucial. Opt for native plant species that thrive in your urban area and are beneficial to bees and other pollinators. Diversity is key—mixing flowers that bloom at different times of the year ensures a continuous food source for bees.

Guerrilla Gardening: Reclaiming and Greening Urban Spaces

Guerrilla gardening takes the concept of urban greening a step further by encouraging individuals to plant flowers, shrubs, and trees in neglected public spaces without formal permission. It's a form of eco-activism aimed at transforming unused or unloved plots into thriving green areas.

- **Identifying Sites for Guerrilla Gardening**: Look for spaces that are clearly neglected, such as vacant lots, roadside verges, or barren medians. The goal is to beautify and ecologically enhance these areas, not to encroach on well-maintained spaces or private property.
- **Planting and Maintenance**: Guerrilla gardening can involve more than just seed bombs; it might include planting pollinator-friendly

bushes, setting up small container gardens, or even establishing community vegetable gardens. Remember, the sustainability of these plantings depends on ongoing care, so choose locations where you or your community can regularly tend to the plants.

Legal and Ethical Considerations

While seed bombing and guerrilla gardening are done with positive intentions, they operate in a legal gray area. It's essential to consider the implications of these actions:

- **Respecting the Law**: Understand the local regulations regarding planting in public spaces. In some cases, guerrilla gardening can be seen as vandalism or trespassing, so it's wise to research and potentially seek permission from local authorities.
- **Ethical Planting**: Always use native and non-invasive plant species to avoid ecological imbalances. Consider the potential impacts on local wildlife and the broader ecosystem. The goal is to enhance biodiversity, not to introduce plants that could become the next invasive species.

Seed bombing and guerrilla gardening represent exciting, hands-on approaches to creating more foraging opportunities for urban bees. By engaging in these activities, urban beekeepers and city residents can play a direct role in enhancing the ecological health of their communities, fostering a richer, more diverse urban landscape for pollinators and people alike.

Volunteering and Community Engagement

Engaging in volunteer work and community initiatives can significantly amplify the impact urban beekeepers have on their local ecosystems and the broader urban environment. This part of the chapter focuses on how beekeepers can extend their passion for beekeeping into community service, advocating for bee-friendly policies, and fostering a culture of environmental stewardship. Here's how to get involved and make a difference:

Volunteering with Environmental Groups and City Committees

- **Finding Your Fit**: Start by researching local environmental groups, gardening clubs, and city planning committees focused on sustainability and urban greening. Many cities have organizations dedicated to increasing green spaces and promoting biodiversity.
- **Leveraging Your Expertise**: As a beekeeper, you bring valuable knowledge about pollinators and their needs. Offer your expertise to help design pollinator-friendly urban spaces or to educate others about the importance of bees in our ecosystems.
- **Advocating for Change**: Use your voice within these groups to advocate for bee-friendly policies. This could include lobbying for the planting of native, bee-attracting flora in public spaces, reducing pesticide use, or creating protected habitats for pollinators.

Organizing Community Planting Days

- **Planning Your Event**: Coordinate with local authorities, community centers, or environmental groups to organize planting days. Focus on selecting locations that could benefit from increased pollinator-friendly plants, such as parks, schoolyards, or neglected urban areas.
- **Engagement and Education**: These events are excellent opportunities to engage the community and educate participants about the importance of bees. Prepare informative materials or short talks to share during the event, highlighting how everyone can contribute to supporting urban pollinators.
- **Logistics and Resources**: Ensure you have all the necessary permissions and resources. This includes plants, gardening tools, and safety equipment. Partner with local nurseries or gardening centers that might be willing to donate supplies or offer discounts for community projects.

©Anthony Carter | www.beekeeping-101.com |part of Carman Online Content Publishing Ltd

Hosting Educational Events and Workshops

- **Workshop Topics**: Organize workshops on topics such as beekeeping basics, creating bee-friendly gardens, or the role of bees in our food system. Tailor the content to your audience, whether it's school children, community members, or fellow urban gardeners.
- **Collaboration for Broader Reach**: Collaborate with libraries, community centers, or educational institutions to host these events. They can help with logistics, promotion, and providing a venue.
- **Interactive and Engaging Format**: Make your workshops interactive by including hands-on activities, such as building bee hotels, planting seeds, or even a demonstration hive (if feasible). This hands-on approach makes learning memorable and enjoyable.

Benefits of Community Engagement

- **Strengthening Networks**: Volunteering and organizing community events not only benefit the bees but also help build stronger, more connected communities. They foster a sense of collective responsibility towards our environment and create networks of like-minded individuals passionate about making a difference.
- **Empowering Others**: By sharing your knowledge and enthusiasm, you empower others to take action. Each person who plants a bee-friendly flower or reduces their pesticide use contributes to a healthier urban ecosystem for bees and other pollinators.
- **Creating Impactful Change**: Collectively, these efforts can lead to significant environmental improvements. Urban areas can transform into thriving habitats for bees, showcasing how cities can coexist with and support natural ecosystems.

Through volunteering and community engagement, urban beekeepers can play a pivotal role in transforming cities into pollinator-friendly environments. These initiatives not only enhance urban foraging for bees, but also contribute to building resilient, informed, and engaged communities dedicated to sustainability and biodiversity.

Chapter 7: Harvesting and Using Urban Honey

This chapter will guide you through the delightful journey from hive to table, revealing the nuances of collecting honey in city environments. This chapter not only provides a step-by-step approach to ethically and safely harvest honey from your urban hives but also explores the myriad ways to utilize this golden elixir and the beeswax byproduct. From the initial extraction to the creative culinary and craft applications, we'll delve into the practices that make urban honey unique. Whether you're a seasoned beekeeper or a novice eager to taste the fruits of your labor, this chapter offers valuable insights into making the most of your urban beekeeping experience, ensuring your efforts contribute positively to the urban ecosystem and your community.

Harvesting Honey in Urban Environments

Timing Your Harvest

Urban areas are teeming with diverse plant species, from parkland trees to rooftop gardens, each with its own flowering schedule. These bloom cycles directly influence the availability of nectar for your bees and, consequently, the timing and quantity of your honey harvest. To effectively time your harvest, consider the following factors:

- **Local Bloom Cycles:** Familiarize yourself with the flowering periods of nectar-producing plants in your area. Urban beekeepers can benefit from the extended blooming seasons common in cities, thanks to a wide variety of ornamental and garden plants. Keeping a bloom calendar can help you predict when your bees will have the most forage available and, thus, when they'll be producing the most honey.

- **Monitoring Hive Activity:** Observing your bees can provide valuable clues about the right time to harvest. Increased activity around the hive entrance, especially bees returning with full pollen baskets, can indicate peak nectar flow. Conversely, a noticeable decrease in foraging activity might signal the end of a bloom cycle, suggesting that it's time to check if your honey is ready for extraction.
- **Inspecting Honey Frames:** Regular hive inspections are crucial for determining if your honey is ripe. A frame ready for harvest should be about 80% capped with wax, indicating that the honey has been dehydrated to the appropriate moisture content by the bees. Harvesting too early can lead to honey that's too high in moisture, which may ferment during storage.
- **Colony Health and Strength:** The well-being of your bee colony is paramount. Ensure that your bees have enough honey reserves to sustain themselves, particularly if you're harvesting late in the season. A strong, healthy colony is more capable of replenishing its stores after a harvest, but always leave enough honey for the bees to overwinter successfully.

Timing your harvest with these considerations in mind not only maximizes your yield, but also safeguards the health of your bees. By aligning your beekeeping practices with the natural cycles of your urban environment, you contribute to a sustainable ecosystem, both for your bees and the community at large.

Safe and Ethical Harvesting Practices

Harvesting honey from your urban hives is a rewarding culmination of your beekeeping efforts, but it's crucial to approach this process with care and respect for the well-being of your bees. Here are guidelines to ensure safe and ethical harvesting practices that prioritize the health of your bee colony and the sustainability of your urban beekeeping practice:

- **Minimize Stress on Bees**: Always approach your hive calmly and gently to minimize stress on the bees. Use a smoker sparingly to soothe the bees before you begin the harvest. The smoke mimics a natural signal of an impending fire, encouraging bees to consume honey and become less aggressive, making it safer for both you and the bees during the harvest.

- **Harvest at the Right Time**: Timing is everything when it comes to harvesting honey. Ensure that there is ample forage available for the bees to replenish their stores after you've taken honey. Late spring through early fall is typically the best time to harvest, as flowers are in bloom and bees are most active. Avoid harvesting too late in the season when bees need their honey stores for winter.
- **Leave Enough Honey for the Bees**: A critical aspect of ethical beekeeping is ensuring that your bees have enough honey to sustain themselves, especially through the winter months. As a rule of thumb, a colony needs approximately 40 pounds (18 kilograms) of honey to survive the winter, but this can vary based on your local climate. Always leave more honey in the hive than you think the bees will need.
- **Use Non-Invasive Harvesting Techniques**: Employ harvesting methods that are least disruptive to the bees. Techniques such as the use of a bee escape board can gently encourage bees to vacate the honey supers, minimizing disturbance during the harvest. Avoid shaking or brushing bees off the frames aggressively, as this can stress or harm them.
- **Ensure Hive Health Before and After Harvest**: Inspect your hive for signs of disease or pests before proceeding with the harvest. Harvesting from a weak or sick colony can further stress the bees and exacerbate any existing conditions. After the harvest, monitor the hive closely to ensure it recovers well and the bees resume their normal activities.
- **Educate Yourself and Stay Informed**: Ethical beekeeping practices evolve with new research and insights into bee behavior and health. Stay informed about best practices by engaging with local beekeeping communities, attending workshops, and reading up-to-date resources on sustainable beekeeping.

If you adhere to these safe and ethical harvesting practices, as an urban beekeeper you can ensure the well-being of your bee colonies while enjoying the sweet rewards of your labor. Ethical harvesting not only supports the sustainability of your urban beekeeping endeavor but also contributes to the overall health of the urban ecosystem, showcasing the harmonious balance between human activities and nature.

Tools and Equipment for Harvesting

Harvesting honey in an urban setting requires not just skill and knowledge, but also the right set of tools and equipment. These tools make the extraction process efficient, safe for the bees, and suitable for the often-limited spaces of city beekeeping. Here's an overview of the essential gear every urban beekeeper should have on hand for honey harvesting season.

Honey Extractors

- **Types of Extractors:** Honey extractors come in manual and electric models. Manual extractors are ideal for urban beekeepers with a small number of hives, as they're more affordable and require minimal space. Electric extractors, while more expensive, can save time and effort if you're managing multiple hives.
- **Choosing the Right Size:** Consider the size of your operation and your storage space. A two-frame manual extractor is compact and perfect for the hobbyist, while larger, more advanced models might suit urban beekeepers with more space and more hives.

Uncapping Tools

- **Uncapping Knives:** An essential tool for removing the thin layer of wax that seals the honey within each cell of the comb. Electric uncapping knives, which heat up to melt the wax more easily, offer efficiency but require access to electricity. A simple, non-electric uncapping knife can also do the job effectively.
- **Uncapping Forks:** For beekeepers who prefer a more hands-on approach or need to uncap irregular surfaces that a knife can't reach, uncapping forks are invaluable. They allow for precise control and are excellent for getting into tight spaces.

Filters and Strainers

- **Purpose and Types:** After extraction, honey often contains bits of wax, propolis, and possibly other debris that need to be removed. Filters and strainers come in various sizes and mesh grades to clean your honey to the desired clarity.
- **Choosing Filters:** For urban beekeepers, space-saving options like collapsible silicone strainers or multi-use mesh filters that fit over your bottling bucket are practical choices. They're effective, easy to store, and versatile enough for different stages of filtering.

Additional Tools

- **Bee Brush:** Gently encourages bees to leave the comb without harm, essential during the harvest.
- **Bottling Buckets:** Equipped with a spigot at the bottom, these buckets make transferring your filtered honey into storage jars or bottles a clean and easy process.
- **Hive Tool:** A multi-purpose tool for prying apart hive boxes and frames, scraping off excess wax or propolis, and aiding in the harvest process.

Considerations for Urban Beekeepers

Urban beekeepers must consider their space limitations and the proximity to neighbors when selecting their equipment. Compact, multi-functional tools that can be easily stored and cleaned are ideal. Noise levels are also a consideration, especially for those using electric extractors in shared spaces or residential areas.

Choosing the right tools and equipment for honey harvesting in an urban environment not only facilitates a smoother, more enjoyable harvesting process, but also ensures the well-being of your bees and the quality of your honey. With careful selection and maintenance of your harvesting gear, you can look forward to many seasons of successful and rewarding urban beekeeping.

©Anthony Carter | www.beekeeping-101.com |part of Carman Online Content Publishing Ltd

Processing and Storing Urban Honey

Extracting Honey

Extracting honey from the comb is a rewarding culmination of your urban beekeeping efforts. Whether you're using manual or mechanical extractors, the process requires careful handling to ensure the quality of the honey while keeping the integrity of the comb for future use by your bees. Here's a step-by-step guide tailored for small-scale urban beekeeping operations:

1. **Preparation**
   - **Gather Your Tools**: Ensure you have an uncapping knife or fork, an extractor (manual or electric, depending on your scale), and containers for the extracted honey.
   - **Suit Up**: Wear protective gear to avoid any bee stings during the process. Even though you'll be working primarily with the combs, it's best to be cautious.
   - **Choose the Right Time and Place**: Extracting honey can be sticky and attract bees, so choose a calm day and a location away from your bee hives, ideally in a space that's easy to clean.

2. **Uncapping the Honeycomb**
   - **Uncapping**: Use the uncapping knife or fork to gently remove the wax cap from each cell on the honeycomb. An uncapping tray can catch the wax and any honey drips, minimizing waste.
   - **Temperature Matters**: Warm honey flows more easily. If the ambient temperature is low, consider gently warming the frames in a honey warmer or a warm room to make uncapping and extraction easier.

3. **Loading the Extractor**
   - **Insert Frames**: Place the uncapped frames into the extractor. If using a manual extractor, balance the load by placing frames opposite each other.

- **Securing the Frames**: Ensure the frames are securely fastened within the extractor to prevent damage during the spinning process.

4. **Extraction**
   - **Manual Extractor**: If using a manual extractor, turn the handle steadily. Start slowly to avoid breaking the frames and gradually increase speed until honey begins to flow out.
   - **Electric Extractor**: For electric extractors, set the speed according to the manufacturer's instructions and watch as the honey is spun out of the combs.

5. **Collecting the Honey**
   - **Drain the Honey**: Once extraction is complete, open the tap at the bottom of the extractor and let the honey flow into a bucket or container fitted with a strainer to catch any wax particles.
   - **Filtering**: Further filter the honey through a fine mesh to remove smaller impurities, ensuring a clear product. Avoid over-filtering to preserve natural pollen and enzymes in the honey.

6. **Resting**
   - **Let the Honey Settle**: Allow the honey to settle for a day or two. This process helps air bubbles rise to the top and can be skimmed off, improving the clarity and quality of the final product.

7. **Bottling**
   - **Prepare Containers**: Ensure your containers are clean and dry. Glass jars are ideal for long-term storage of honey, as they don't impart any flavors or chemicals.
   - **Filling Jars**: Use a honey gate or a ladle to fill your jars with honey, leaving a small space at the top. Seal tightly.

8. **Cleanup**
   - **Wax and Equipment**: Clean your tools and extractor with warm water. The wax cappings can be melted down and used for candles or other beeswax products, ensuring nothing goes to waste.

Extracting honey is both an art and a science, requiring patience and practice. By following these steps, urban beekeepers can efficiently harvest their honey, ensuring the wellbeing of their bees and the quality of the honey produced. This process not only rewards you with a sweet harvest but also deepens your connection to your urban beekeeping practice.

Filtering and Bottling

After successfully extracting honey from your hives, the next crucial steps are filtering and bottling, which ensure your honey is ready for consumption, storage, or sale. These processes not only enhance the aesthetic appeal of your honey, but also its quality and longevity. Here's how to approach filtering and bottling your urban honey effectively.

Filtering Honey

Filtering is essential to remove wax, dead bees, and other impurities from your honey, leaving you with a clear and pure product. Here are some tips for effective filtering:

- **Choose the Right Filter**: Filters come in various sizes and materials. A double-strainer setup, with a coarse filter on top and a fine mesh below, is ideal for urban beekeepers. This setup allows you to efficiently remove large particles first, followed by finer impurities.
- **Warm Honey for Easier Filtering**: Gently warming your honey (not exceeding 104°F or 40°C to preserve natural enzymes) can make it easier to filter. Warm honey flows more freely through filters, speeding up the process while ensuring the honey retains its natural qualities.
- **Filtering Process**: Place your chosen filter(s) over a clean, food-grade bucket or container. Slowly pour the extracted honey through the filters. Patience is key; allow the honey to pass through the filters gradually. If the honey is warmed, ensure it's done evenly to avoid overheating any portion.

Bottling Honey

Bottling is the final step in preparing your honey for storage or sale. This step is not just functional but also an opportunity to showcase your honey's urban origin.

- **Choosing Containers**: Glass jars and bottles are popular choices for honey because of their non-reactive nature and ability to be sterilized. Plastic containers specifically designed for food storage can also be used, especially if you're planning to sell or transport your honey. Consider the size of the containers based on how you intend to use or sell the honey.
- **Sterilizing Containers**: Ensure all containers and lids are thoroughly sterilized before bottling your honey. This can be done by boiling them in water for 10 minutes or using a dishwasher with a sanitizing cycle. Sterilization is crucial to prevent contamination and prolong the shelf life of your honey.
- **Filling Containers**: Use a clean, sterilized funnel to fill your containers with honey, leaving a small space at the top to allow for easy closing. Ensure the process is done in a clean environment to maintain the purity of the honey.
- **Labeling Your Honey**: Labels are not just a legal requirement; they are also an opportunity to tell the story of your urban honey. Include essential information like the bottling date and net weight. Additionally, highlight your honey's urban origin, perhaps mentioning the city or neighborhood and the types of local flowers your bees forage. This not only adds a unique selling point, but also connects consumers to their local environment.
- **Legal Requirements**: If you plan to sell your honey, research and comply with local labeling regulations. These might include nutritional information, your contact details, and any required health warnings.

Filtering and bottling are the final touches in preparing your urban honey for enjoyment. By following these steps, you ensure that the quality of the honey reflects the care and effort you've put into your urban beekeeping

©Anthony Carter | www.beekeeping-101.com |part of Carman Online Content Publishing Ltd

endeavor, offering a clear, pure product that's a true testament to the unique environment from which it came.

Storing Honey

Once you've harvested and processed your urban honey, proper storage is crucial to maintain its quality and extend its shelf life. Honey is a natural product that, when stored correctly, can remain stable for years, if not indefinitely. However, its longevity and quality can be affected by factors such as temperature, moisture, and light. Here's how to ensure your urban honey stays as fresh and delicious as the day it was harvested:

Ideal Storage Conditions

- **Temperature:** The best temperature to store honey is between 50°F to 70°F (10°C to 21°C). Extreme temperatures, either too hot or too cold, can affect honey's texture and flavor. High temperatures can lead to honey darkening and losing its aroma and flavor, while too cold temperatures can accelerate crystallization.
- **Light:** Honey should be stored in a dark place away from direct sunlight. Light can degrade honey's quality, leading to color changes and possible loss of nutrients.
- **Moisture:** Ensure honey is stored in an airtight container to prevent moisture absorption. Honey naturally attracts moisture, which can lead to fermentation and spoilage if not properly sealed.

Containers for Honey Storage

- **Glass Jars:** Glass jars are ideal for storing honey as they do not impart any flavors and are airtight, keeping moisture out. They also protect honey from light if stored in a cupboard or pantry.
- **Plastic Containers:** Food-grade plastic containers can also be used, especially for larger quantities. Ensure they are specifically designed for food storage to prevent any chemicals from leaching into the honey.

- **Avoid Metal Containers:** Metal can react with honey, leading to oxidation and deterioration of the honey's quality. Stick to glass or food-grade plastic for long-term storage.

Handling Crystallization

Crystallization is a natural process where glucose in honey precipitates into solid crystals. It doesn't indicate spoilage but changes the texture, making it thick and grainy. Here's how to handle it:

- **Preventing Crystallization:** Keeping honey at stable temperatures can slow down crystallization. However, some honey types crystallize faster than others due to their natural sugar composition.
- **Reversing Crystallization:** If your honey crystallizes, gently warm it to dissolve the crystals. Place the honey container in a warm water bath, ensuring the water temperature is not too hot to avoid damaging the honey's natural properties. Avoid using a microwave as it can unevenly heat and potentially spoil the honey.

By following these storage tips, you can enjoy your urban honey's natural sweetness and health benefits for years. Remember, the key to successful honey storage is to keep it in an airtight container, at a stable temperature, away from direct light and moisture. This ensures your honey remains a flavorful and nutritious addition to your pantry, ready to be used whenever you need a touch of sweetness.

Creative Uses for Honey and Beeswax

Cooking with Urban Honey

Urban honey, with its unique flavors influenced by the diverse flora of city landscapes, offers a delightful sweetness and complexity to a variety of dishes. Incorporating this golden nectar into your cooking not only enhances the taste of your meals, but also allows you to savor the essence

©Anthony Carter | www.beekeeping-101.com |part of Carman Online Content Publishing Ltd

of your urban environment. Here are some recipes and tips for making the most of your urban honey in the kitchen.

Honey's Role in Cooking

- **Flavor Enhancer**: Urban honey can add depth and richness to both sweet and savory dishes. Its flavor varies based on the local flowers visited by the bees, offering a unique taste of your city's botanical diversity.
- **Natural Sweetener**: Substitute sugar with honey in recipes for a more natural sweetness and a boost of antioxidants.
- **Texture Modifier**: Honey can impart a moist and tender texture to baked goods, making it a perfect addition to cakes, muffins, and bread.

Tips for Cooking with Honey

- **Substituting Sugar with Honey**: When replacing sugar with honey, use about ¾ cup of honey for every 1 cup of sugar, and reduce the amount of liquid in the recipe by ¼ cup to account for honey's moisture content.
- **Temperature Considerations**: Honey's enzymes break down at high temperatures, so adding honey towards the end of the cooking process can help preserve its health benefits and flavors.
- **Balancing Flavors**: The sweetness of honey pairs well with acidic ingredients like lemon or vinegar, enhancing the overall flavor profile of a dish.

Recipe Ideas

Honey Glazed Carrots
- Ingredients: 1lb carrots, peeled and sliced; 2 tbsp olive oil; 4 tbsp urban honey; Salt and pepper to taste.
- Instructions: Toss the carrots in olive oil and roast at 425°F until tender. Drizzle with honey, season with salt and pepper, and roast for an additional 5 minutes.

©Anthony Carter | www.beekeeping-101.com |part of Carman Online Content Publishing Ltd

Urban Honey Vinaigrette

- Ingredients: ¼ cup urban honey, ¼ cup apple cider vinegar, ¾ cup extra virgin olive oil, 1 tsp mustard, salt and pepper to taste.
- Instructions: Whisk together all ingredients until emulsified. Adjust seasoning as needed. Drizzle over your favorite salad.

Honey Lemon Tea

- Ingredients: 1 cup hot water, 1 tbsp urban honey, Juice of ½ lemon.
- Instructions: Stir honey and lemon juice into hot water. Adjust honey or lemon to taste. Perfect for soothing a sore throat or as a comforting warm drink.

Honey and Spice Roasted Nuts

- Ingredients: 2 cups mixed nuts, 2 tbsp urban honey, ½ tsp cinnamon, ¼ tsp cayenne pepper, salt to taste.
- Instructions: Coat nuts in honey and spices. Spread on a baking sheet and roast at 350°F for 10-15 minutes, stirring occasionally, until golden.

Honey Banana Bread

- Ingredients: 2 cups flour, 1 tsp baking soda, ½ tsp salt, ½ cup unsalted butter, ¾ cup urban honey, 2 eggs, 3 ripe bananas mashed, ½ cup walnuts (optional).
- Instructions: Cream together butter and honey. Add eggs, bananas, and dry ingredients. Pour into a loaf pan and bake at 350°F for 60 minutes.

These recipes showcase the versatility of urban honey, transforming simple ingredients into delightful dishes that reflect the unique character of your city's flora. Experiment with your urban honey in various recipes to discover new flavors and textures that celebrate the fruits of your beekeeping endeavors.

Homemade Beeswax Products

Beeswax, a natural byproduct of honey production, is a versatile and valuable resource for urban beekeepers. Rich in texture and with a pleasant, subtle aroma, beeswax can be transformed into a variety of sustainable products, from candles to cosmetics. This section provides instructions for creating your own beeswax products, allowing you to utilize every aspect of your harvest and minimize waste.

Beeswax Candles

Materials Needed:
- Beeswax (either in block form or pastilles)
- Candle wicks
- Double boiler or a similar setup for melting wax
- Molds or containers for candles
- Thermometer (optional but recommended)

Instructions:
1. **Prepare Your Molds:** If using molds, ensure they are clean and dry. Attach the wick to the bottom of the mold or container, securing it with a bit of melted wax or an adhesive.
2. **Melt the Beeswax:** Place beeswax in the top part of a double boiler, heating it slowly until completely melted. Avoid overheating to preserve the quality of the wax. Use a thermometer to monitor the temperature, aiming for about 145-150°F (63-66°C).
3. **Pour the Wax:** Once melted, carefully pour the beeswax into your prepared molds or containers, ensuring the wick stays centered.
4. **Cool and Set:** Allow the candles to cool and set completely. This may take several hours or overnight, depending on the size of the candles.
5. **Trim the Wick:** Once the wax has set, trim the wick to about ¼ inch above the wax surface.

Beeswax Cosmetics

Beeswax is a natural emulsifier and is often used in cosmetics for its skin-protecting qualities. Here are simple recipes for making your own beeswax lip balm and lotion bars.

Beeswax Lip Balm:

Materials:
- 2 tablespoons beeswax
- 2 tablespoons coconut oil
- 2 tablespoons shea butter
- Essential oils for fragrance (optional)
- Lip balm tubes or small containers

Instructions:
1. **Melt Ingredients:** Combine beeswax, coconut oil, and shea butter in a double boiler, melting them together over low heat.
2. **Add Essential Oils:** Once melted, remove from heat and stir in a few drops of your chosen essential oils for fragrance.
3. **Pour and Cool:** Carefully pour the mixture into lip balm tubes or containers. Let them cool and solidify before capping.

Beeswax Lotion Bars:

Materials:
- 1 part beeswax
- 1 part coconut oil
- 1 part shea butter
- Molds for shaping bars
- Essential oils (optional)

Instructions:
1. **Melt and Mix:** In a double boiler, melt equal parts of beeswax, coconut oil, and shea butter together.
2. **Customize:** After removing from heat, add a few drops of essential oils if desired.

3. **Mold:** Pour the mixture into molds and allow them to cool and harden.
4. **Use:** Once solidified, pop the bars out of the molds. Rub between your hands or directly on dry skin areas for a moisturizing effect.

Creating beeswax products not only offers a way to engage more deeply with the fruits of your beekeeping, but also provides natural, chemical-free alternatives for everyday items. These projects can serve as personal gifts, a means to further support your beekeeping hobby, or even as the foundation for a small business venture.

Selling Your Honey and Beeswax

Venturing into the world of selling your urban honey and beeswax products is an exciting step for any urban beekeeper. It allows you to share the fruits of your labor with a wider community while promoting urban beekeeping and its benefits. However, navigating this path requires an understanding of local regulations, strategic marketing, and thoughtful packaging to ensure your products stand out in the market. Here's a comprehensive guide to help you successfully sell your urban honey and beeswax products.

Understanding Local Regulations

- **Research Local Laws and Certifications**: Before selling honey and beeswax, familiarize yourself with local health and safety regulations. Many areas require beekeepers to obtain certain certifications or pass health inspections to sell honey legally. Contact your local health department or agricultural extension office for specific requirements.
- **Labeling Requirements**: Proper labeling is crucial. Ensure your labels meet local regulations by including necessary information such as weight, origin (e.g., "Produced in [City Name]"), and a contact number or address. Some regions may also require you to list your honey as a specific type if it meets certain criteria (e.g., "Raw" or "Organic" honey).

Marketing Tips for Urban Beekeepers

- **Tell Your Story**: Urban honey is unique; it tells the story of your city through its flavors and origins. Use this narrative to market your honey, highlighting its urban roots, the types of local plants your bees forage on, and your journey as an urban beekeeper.
- **Utilize Social Media and Online Platforms**: Social media platforms are powerful tools for reaching potential customers. Share engaging content about your beekeeping practices, the benefits of local honey, and behind-the-scenes looks at your harvesting process. Consider setting up an online store or using local online marketplaces to reach a wider audience.
- **Engage with Your Community**: Attend local farmers' markets, craft fairs, and community events to sell your products. Engaging directly with customers allows you to share your passion for beekeeping and educate them on the importance of supporting local bees. Networking with local cafes, restaurants, and shops to stock your honey and beeswax products can also expand your reach.

Packaging and Presenting Your Products

- **Eco-Friendly Packaging**: Choose packaging that reflects the sustainable and natural qualities of your products. Glass jars for honey and recyclable or biodegradable packaging for beeswax items can appeal to eco-conscious consumers.
- **Branding**: Develop a consistent and appealing brand for your products. Include a logo or design that speaks to the urban nature of your honey and beeswax, perhaps incorporating cityscape elements or the specific flowers your bees forage on.
- **Educational Inserts**: Consider including an insert with each product that educates the buyer about the benefits of local honey, the role of bees in urban environments, and tips for using honey and beeswax. This not only adds value to your product, but also fosters a deeper connection between you and your customers.

Selling your urban honey and beeswax is more than a commercial venture; it's an opportunity to advocate for urban beekeeping and contribute to the sustainability of your local environment. By understanding local regulations, employing strategic marketing, and thoughtfully packaging your products, you can successfully share the sweetness of your urban beekeeping efforts with the community.

Promoting Urban Honey

Educating Your Community

Urban honey and beeswax products offer more than just a sweet taste and practical use; they serve as powerful educational tools to highlight the significance of bees in our urban ecosystems. Engaging the community and raising awareness about urban beekeeping can foster a deeper appreciation for these vital pollinators and encourage more sustainable urban living practices. Here are strategies to use your urban honey and beeswax as conduits for education:

Host Honey Tasting Events: Organize events where community members can taste different varieties of honey produced in various parts of the city. Use these gatherings as an opportunity to discuss the nuances of urban beekeeping, the floral sources available in different neighborhoods, and how they influence the flavor profiles of the honey. This sensory experience can spark interest and open discussions about the importance of bees in urban pollination.

Create Educational Packaging: Design your honey jars and beeswax product packaging with educational snippets about urban beekeeping, the role of bees in pollination, and tips for creating bee-friendly environments in the city. QR codes can link to online resources or documentaries about urban beekeeping, offering an interactive learning experience.

Workshops and Demonstrations: Offer workshops or live demonstrations on beekeeping basics, the process of making beeswax products, or cooking with honey. These sessions can be held at local schools, community centers, or even online. They provide hands-on learning experiences, demystifying beekeeping and showcasing its accessibility and benefits to urban communities.

Collaborate with Local Schools: Partner with local schools to incorporate urban beekeeping into their science or environmental education curriculum. Educational programs can include field trips to your apiary, classroom presentations, and interactive projects like building bee hotels or planting bee-friendly gardens. This not only educates the younger generation, but also encourages stewardship of the environment from an early age.

Leverage Social Media: Use social media platforms to share fascinating facts about bees, the beekeeping process, and the challenges and triumphs of urban beekeeping. Regular posts, stories, or live sessions can engage a broader audience, spreading awareness and fostering a community of bee enthusiasts and environmental advocates.

Participate in Community Events: Set up a booth at local farmers' markets, eco-fairs, or community festivals to showcase your honey and beeswax products. Use these opportunities to engage in conversations with attendees about the importance of supporting local beekeepers and the broader environmental benefits of urban beekeeping.

Publish a Blog or Newsletter: Create a blog or newsletter that chronicles your urban beekeeping journey, shares insights into the lives of bees, and offers tips for supporting local pollinators. Regular updates can keep your community informed, engaged, and motivated to contribute positively to the urban ecosystem.

Using these strategies means urban beekeepers can play a pivotal role in educating their communities about the importance of bees and the fascinating world of urban beekeeping. Through engagement and education, we can collectively work towards a more bee-friendly and environmentally conscious urban landscape.

Partnerships with Local Businesses

Creating partnerships with local businesses is a strategic and mutually beneficial way to promote your urban honey while contributing to the sustainability and community spirit of your city. This collaboration not only increases the visibility of urban beekeeping efforts, but also supports local economies and fosters a deeper connection between residents and their food sources. Here are some ideas for engaging with cafes, restaurants, shops, and even local markets to feature your urban honey and create a buzz about beekeeping in your community.

Collaborating with Cafes and Restaurants

- **Feature Your Honey in Menu Items**: Approach local cafes and restaurants with the idea of incorporating your urban honey into their menu. Whether it's a special dessert, a unique salad dressing, or a signature drink, showcasing your honey in delicious dishes can highlight its quality and uniqueness. This not only provides exposure for your product but also offers diners a taste of local flavors.
- **Educational Collaborations**: Work with culinary partners to host educational events that focus on the importance of pollinators and local food sources. These could include honey tastings, cooking demonstrations using honey, or talks on urban beekeeping. Such events can raise awareness about the role of bees in urban environments and promote the use of local ingredients.

Engaging with Local Shops

- **Retail Opportunities**: Partner with local grocery stores, specialty food shops, and gift stores to sell your urban honey. Offering your honey in these settings can reach a wide audience of consumers interested in supporting local producers. Ensure your packaging tells the story of your urban beekeeping journey to connect with customers and differentiate your product.

- **Customized Products for Retailers**: Consider creating exclusive honey blends or beeswax products for specific retailers. This could include special labels that feature the retailer's branding or unique product formulations that are only available at their locations. Such exclusivity can enhance the appeal of your products and strengthen your partnership with the retailer.

Collaborating with Local Markets

- **Farmers' Markets and Artisan Fairs**: Participate in local farmers' markets and artisan fairs to sell your honey directly to the community. These venues offer a platform to engage with consumers, share your beekeeping experiences, and educate the public about the benefits of local honey. It's also an excellent opportunity to network with other local producers and explore potential collaborations.

Creating Buzz Through Promotion

- **Social Media Collaborations**: Leverage social media platforms to promote your partnerships with local businesses. Share stories, photos, and videos that highlight how your honey is being used in dishes, sold in shops, or featured in events. Engaging content can attract a wider audience and drive interest in both your honey and the businesses you're partnered with.
- **Cross-Promotional Marketing**: Engage in cross-promotional marketing efforts with your business partners. This could include joint advertisements, bundled promotions (e.g., a meal at a cafe that comes with a small jar of your honey), or featured articles in local publications. Cross-promotion is a powerful tool for reaching new customers and reinforcing the message of community and sustainability.

If you establish partnerships with local businesses, as an urban beekeeper you can then significantly enhance the visibility and appeal of your honey, underscore the significance of urban beekeeping, and contribute to a vibrant, sustainable local food system. These collaborations not only benefit your beekeeping endeavors but also strengthen community ties and support the local economy, creating a win-win situation for everyone involved.

Challenges and Solutions

Dealing with Contaminants

Urban environments, while offering unique opportunities for beekeeping, also present specific challenges in terms of potential contaminants that may affect honey quality. These contaminants can range from pollutants in the air and water to chemicals used in urban landscaping and agricultural practices within city limits. Understanding these risks and knowing how to test for and mitigate them is crucial for ensuring the safety and purity of your urban honey.

Identifying Potential Contaminants

- **Air and Water Pollution:** Urban areas can have higher levels of air and water pollution, including particulates from vehicles and industrial activities. These pollutants can be deposited on flowers, which bees then visit, potentially transferring contaminants to the honey.
- **Chemical Exposure:** Pesticides, herbicides, and fungicides used in urban gardens, parks, and green spaces can pose risks to bees and their honey. Bees collecting nectar and pollen from treated plants may bring these chemicals back to the hive.
- **Heavy Metals:** Urban soils can contain heavy metals like lead, cadmium, and arsenic, remnants of industrial activities or historical use of contaminated products. Plants grown in these soils can absorb these metals, which can then be transferred to bees and their honey.

Testing for Contaminants

- **Laboratory Analysis:** Regular testing of honey samples for common contaminants is an essential practice for urban beekeepers. Many local agricultural extension offices or environmental laboratories offer testing services for honey. These tests can screen for a range of substances, including heavy metals, pesticides, and other chemical residues.
- **Hive Location Assessments:** Conducting environmental assessments of potential hive locations can help identify areas with lower risk of contamination. Choosing sites away from heavy traffic, industrial zones, and known sources of pollution can reduce the risk of contaminant exposure.

Mitigation Strategies

- **Strategic Hive Placement:** Positioning hives in areas with lower exposure to pollutants and away from treated plants can significantly reduce the risk of contamination. Rooftops, enclosed gardens, and areas with abundant native flora offer safer foraging options for urban bees.
- **Community Engagement:** Working with local communities, parks, and garden clubs to promote the use of bee-friendly and organic gardening practices can help reduce the overall chemical load in the urban environment. Encouraging the planting of diverse, native plants also supports healthier foraging options for bees.
- **Regular Monitoring and Management:** Keeping a close eye on bee behavior and hive health can offer early warning signs of potential contamination issues. Implementing integrated pest management strategies within the hive can reduce the need for chemical treatments, further ensuring the purity of your honey.

The challenge of dealing with contaminants in urban honey is significant but manageable with informed strategies and proactive measures. Through testing, strategic hive placement, and community engagement, urban beekeepers can mitigate the risks of contamination, ensuring their honey remains a safe, pure, and enjoyable product. By understanding and addressing these challenges, urban beekeepers contribute positively to the health of their bees, the quality of their honey, and the sustainability of urban ecosystems.

Managing Limited Harvests

Urban beekeeping often comes with its unique set of challenges, not least of which is the potential for limited honey harvests. The constraints of space, varying forage availability, and the impact of urban microclimates can all influence the productivity of your hives. However, with strategic planning and management, you can maximize honey production, even in the most compact of city environments. Here are some tips for overcoming these challenges and ensuring a sustainable approach to urban beekeeping.

Optimize Hive Placement

- **Sunlight and Shade:** Position your hives in areas that receive ample morning sunlight but are shaded during the hottest part of the day. This balance promotes active foraging while preventing overheating.
- **Wind Protection:** Use barriers such as walls or shrubbery to protect hives from strong winds, which can discourage bees from foraging.
- **Elevation:** Consider rooftop or elevated placements to give bees direct flight paths to foraging areas, reducing their energy expenditure and increasing productivity.

Enhance Forage Availability

- **Plant Bee-Friendly Flora:** Even in urban settings, you can enhance local forage by planting bee-friendly plants on balconies, rooftops, and communal gardens. Opt for a variety of species that bloom at different times to provide a consistent food source.
- **Collaborate with Community:** Work with local parks, community gardens, and green spaces to encourage the planting of pollinator-

friendly plants. Increasing the overall forage availability supports not just your bees but the broader urban bee population.

- **Supplemental Feeding:** In seasons when natural forage is scarce, consider supplemental feeding with sugar syrup or pollen substitutes. This should be done judiciously to avoid dependency and promote natural foraging behaviors.

Manage Hive Health and Stress

- **Regular Inspections:** Keep a close eye on your hives to manage pests, diseases, and stressors promptly. Healthy bees are more productive and better equipped to cope with urban challenges.
- **Minimize Disturbances:** Urban environments can be bustling. Position your hives in quieter, less disturbed areas, and when possible, schedule your hive inspections during less active periods to reduce stress on the colony.

Utilize Swarm Management Techniques

- **Splitting Hives:** Proactively splitting hives before they swarm can not only prevent loss of bees but can increase your overall honey production by establishing more colonies.
- **Queen Management:** Requeening with queens bred for high productivity and gentleness can improve the overall efficiency of your hive, leading to better honey yields.

Educate and Engage the Community

- **Advocate for Bee-Friendly Policies:** Work with local governments and organizations to promote bee-friendly policies that enhance urban foraging landscapes.
- **Community Engagement:** Educating your community about the importance of bees can lead to more green spaces and foraging opportunities, indirectly benefiting your beekeeping efforts.

Adopting these strategies means urban beekeepers can overcome the limitations of their environment and enjoy fruitful harvests. Remember, every small effort contributes to a larger impact, both for your hives and the urban ecosystem they support.

Chapter 8: Community Engagement and Education

Urban beekeeping is not just about managing hives and harvesting honey; it's a practice that thrives on community involvement and education. This chapter delves into the importance of building a supportive network, engaging in educational outreach, and collaborating with local businesses and organizations to foster a bee-friendly city environment. As urban beekeepers, we have the unique opportunity to act as ambassadors for bees, educating others about their vital role in our ecosystems and advocating for practices that support pollinator health. By fostering community connections, we can create a more inclusive and informed urban beekeeping community, leading to sustainable practices that benefit both bees and people. Whether you're looking to start a beekeeping club, take part in local outreach, or collaborate with businesses for mutual benefits, this chapter provides the tools and insights needed to make a positive impact in your community.

Building a Supportive Urban Beekeeping Community

Starting or Joining a Local Beekeeping Club

Urban beekeeping, by its nature, presents a unique set of challenges and rewards, making the support of a community not just beneficial but essential for success. Whether you're taking your first steps into the world of beekeeping or you're an experienced beekeeper adapting to the urban environment, joining a local beekeeping club can significantly enhance your journey. These clubs offer a platform for support, shared resources, knowledge exchange, and sometimes even collaborative projects that can have a broader impact on the local ecosystem and community.

©Anthony Carter | www.beekeeping-101.com | part of Carman Online Content Publishing Ltd

Benefits of Joining a Local Beekeeping Club

- **Knowledge Sharing:** Beekeeping clubs are treasure troves of collective wisdom, where members, ranging from novices to experts, share insights, experiences, and best practices. This exchange of knowledge is invaluable, especially when facing the unique challenges of urban beekeeping.
- **Shared Resources:** Many clubs provide access to shared resources such as equipment, books, and even spaces for meetings or workshops. This can be particularly helpful for beginners who are still in the process of acquiring their own tools and resources.
- **Mentorship Opportunities:** Having a mentor can drastically shorten your learning curve in beekeeping. Experienced beekeepers can provide guidance, answer questions, and offer hands-on assistance. Mentorship within a club setting fosters a sense of camaraderie and support.
- **Community Projects:** Many beekeeping clubs engage in community projects such as creating pollinator gardens, organizing educational programs in schools, or advocating for bee-friendly policies. Participating in these projects can be rewarding and amplify the positive impact of your beekeeping activities.
- **Networking:** Being part of a club allows you to connect with individuals who share your interests. These connections can lead to friendships, collaborations, and even partnerships that extend beyond beekeeping.

Finding an Existing Beekeeping Club

The first step to joining a local beekeeping club is to search for existing ones in your area. Many cities and towns have their own beekeeping associations that welcome new members. You can start by:

- Searching online for "beekeeping clubs near me" or "urban beekeeping associations."

- Visiting local garden centers or agricultural supply stores, as they often have information on local beekeeping groups.

- Checking community boards or social media platforms where local environmental or gardening groups may post.

Starting Your Own Beekeeping Club

If you discover that there isn't a beekeeping club in your area, or if existing clubs don't focus on the specific challenges of urban beekeeping, starting your own club can be a fantastic way to build a community. Here are some steps to consider:

- **Identify Interest:** Begin by identifying other beekeepers in your area or people interested in starting. You can use social media, community boards, or local events to gauge interest.
- **Organize an Initial Meeting:** Plan an informal meeting to discuss goals, interests, and the potential structure of the club. This can be done online or in a local community space.
- **Set Objectives:** Clearly define the club's objectives, whether they're focused on education, advocacy, community projects, or all of the above.
- **Promote Your Club:** Use social media, local community boards, and word of mouth to promote your club and attract members.
- **Regular Meetings and Activities:** Establish a schedule for regular meetings and plan activities that will benefit members, such as guest speakers, workshops, and field trips.

Building or joining a beekeeping club can significantly enrich your urban beekeeping experience, providing a supportive network that fosters learning, collaboration, and community engagement. Whether you're looking to share your experiences, learn from others, or contribute to local sustainability efforts, a beekeeping club is a valuable resource for every urban beekeeper.

Networking and Mentorship Opportunities

For novice urban beekeepers, the journey into beekeeping can be as daunting as it is exciting. The complexity of managing a hive, coupled with the unique challenges of urban environments, can make the early stages of beekeeping seem overwhelming. This is where the value of mentorship and networking becomes unmistakable. Experienced beekeepers possess a wealth of knowledge and practical insights that can significantly ease the learning curve for beginners. By sharing their experiences, successes, and failures, mentors can provide invaluable guidance that textbooks and online resources alone cannot offer.

Mentorship in urban beekeeping goes beyond simple advice on hive management. It encompasses navigating local regulations, understanding urban foraging patterns, and even mediating neighborly concerns. A mentor can offer personalized advice tailored to the specific conditions of your urban setting, helping you to make informed decisions and avoid common pitfalls. This one-on-one support can be instrumental in building confidence and ensuring the welfare of your bees and the community.

Networking within the beekeeping community is equally important. It opens doors to a broader spectrum of knowledge, experiences, and perspectives. Urban beekeepers can benefit from joining local beekeeping clubs, associations, or online forums where they can share stories, exchange tips, and stay updated on beekeeping practices and scientific research. Events such as workshops, seminars, and beekeeping conferences serve as excellent platforms for networking. These gatherings not only enhance your beekeeping skills and knowledge but also strengthen the sense of community among urban beekeepers.

Several platforms facilitate networking and mentorship opportunities for urban beekeepers:

- **Local Beekeeping Associations:** Many cities have local beekeeping clubs or associations that welcome members of all experience levels. These groups often host regular meetings, educational talks, and hive visits.

- **Online Forums and Social Media Groups:** Digital platforms like Beekeeping forums and social media groups offer a space for beekeepers to connect, ask questions, and share advice from anywhere in the world.
- **Beekeeping Workshops and Conferences:** Participating in workshops and attending beekeeping conferences can provide hands-on learning experiences and the chance to meet experienced beekeepers and industry experts.
- **Community Gardens and Environmental Organizations:** Engaging with community gardens and local environmental groups can provide networking opportunities with individuals interested in sustainability and pollination.

Fostering mentorship and networking within the urban beekeeping community means beekeepers can create a supportive environment that encourages learning, collaboration, and mutual support. This collective wisdom not only benefits individual beekeepers and their hives, but also contributes to the broader goal of promoting bee health and sustainability in urban environments.

Creating a Buzz on Social Media

In today's digital age, social media is a powerful tool for building communities and spreading awareness on various issues, including urban beekeeping. By leveraging platforms like Instagram, Facebook, Twitter, and even YouTube, urban beekeepers can create a buzz around their activities, share their stories of success and challenge, and engage in important discussions about bee conservation and sustainable urban living. Here are some tips for using social media to enhance your urban beekeeping community:

- **Share Your Story**: Every beekeeper has a unique journey. Use your social media platforms to share how you got started, the challenges you've faced, and the successes you've celebrated. Personal stories resonate with people and can inspire others to take an interest in beekeeping or support bee conservation efforts.

- **Educational Content**: Use your platform to educate your followers about bees and beekeeping. Post facts about bee biology, the importance of pollinators, and tips for creating bee-friendly environments. Videos and photos from your own beekeeping practice can be especially engaging and informative.
- **Engage with Your Audience**: Social media is not just about broadcasting; it's about engaging. Respond to comments, ask your followers questions, and encourage them to share their thoughts and experiences. This two-way interaction fosters a sense of community and involvement.
- **Collaborate with Influencers and Organizations**: Partner with influencers and organizations that share your passion for sustainability and conservation. These collaborations can help you reach a wider audience and amplify your message. Look for local environmental groups, gardening clubs, and even other beekeepers to cross-promote content.
- **Use Hashtags Wisely**: Hashtags can increase the visibility of your posts. Use popular beekeeping and conservation-related hashtags, as well as local hashtags specific to your city or community. This makes it easier for like-minded individuals to find and engage with your content.
- **Highlight Community Involvement**: Showcase any community events, workshops, or talks you're involved in. Sharing these experiences can encourage others to take part in future events, strengthening the urban beekeeping community.
- **Advocate for Change**: Use your platform to advocate for policies and practices that support bee health and urban beekeeping. Whether it's promoting pesticide-free gardens or supporting urban green spaces, social media can be a powerful tool for change.

Creating a vibrant community around urban beekeeping on social media not only raises awareness but also provides a supportive network for beekeepers. Through consistent engagement, educational content, and advocacy, you can contribute to a greater understanding and appreciation of bees in the urban environment, encouraging more sustainable practices and policies for their protection.

Educational Outreach Programs

Workshops, Seminars, and School Programs

Educating the public about the importance of bees and beekeeping is crucial for building a sustainable future for urban beekeeping. Workshops, seminars, and school programs offer effective platforms for spreading knowledge, fostering appreciation, and inspiring action among community members of all ages. Here's how to organize and deliver impactful educational outreach programs.

Organizing Workshops and Seminars

Identify Your Objectives:
- Determine the key messages you want to convey, such as the role of bees in pollination, the basics of beekeeping, or the importance of creating pollinator-friendly environments.
- Tailor your content to suit the audience's level of knowledge and interest.

Select the Venue:
- Choose a venue that is accessible and appealing to your target audience. Community centers, public libraries, and local parks with green spaces are excellent options.
- Consider virtual platforms for wider reach and accessibility.

Engage Expert Speakers:
- Invite experienced beekeepers, entomologists, or environmental educators to share their knowledge and experiences.
- Include a Q&A session to encourage audience participation and engagement.

Provide Hands-On Experience:
- If possible, include a practical component, such as a visit to a local hive or a demonstration of beekeeping equipment.

- Hands-on activities are especially effective in capturing interest and enhancing learning.

Promote Your Event:
- Use social media, local community boards, and partnerships with environmental organizations to advertise your event.
- Reach out to local media for coverage to increase visibility.

Partnering with Schools

Introduce Beekeeping and Pollination Concepts:
- Develop age-appropriate materials that introduce children to the world of bees and their role in our ecosystem.
- Use engaging tools like storytelling, games, and interactive presentations to capture the students' interest.

Collaborate with Educators:
- Work with teachers to integrate beekeeping and pollination topics into the curriculum, aligning with subjects like science, environmental studies, and even art.
- Offer resources and support for teachers to continue the conversation in the classroom.

Organize Field Trips and School Visits:
- Coordinate visits to local hives or invite beekeepers to bring equipment and educational materials to the school.
- Ensure safety by adhering to guidelines for interacting with bees and using protective gear.

Create Bee-Friendly School Projects:
- Encourage schools to participate in projects that support bee populations, such as planting pollinator gardens or building bee hotels.
- These projects can be integrated into the school's environmental club activities or science classes.

©Anthony Carter | www.beekeeping-101.com |part of Carman Online Content Publishing Ltd

Foster Youth Beekeeping Clubs:
- Help establish beekeeping clubs in schools or community centers to provide ongoing education and hands-on experience for interested students.
- Support these clubs with resources, mentorship, and opportunities for community engagement.

By implementing these strategies, urban beekeepers can play a pivotal role in educating the public and inspiring the next generation of bee enthusiasts. Educational outreach programs not only raise awareness about the importance of bees but also build a community of informed and engaged citizens ready to support urban beekeeping initiatives.

Creating Educational Materials and Resources

One of the most effective ways to engage and inform your community about the importance of bees and urban beekeeping is through the development of educational materials and resources. These materials can serve as vital tools to spread awareness, dispel myths, and ignite interest in pollinator conservation among people of all ages. Here's how to create engaging, informative, and accessible educational content.

Understand Your Audience: Before creating any materials, it's crucial to identify your target audience. Are you aiming to educate school children, local gardeners, or the general public? Understanding your audience will guide the tone, complexity, and type of content you create. For children, materials should be colorful, engaging, and simplified. For adults, you can delve into more complex topics but still keep the content accessible and interesting.

Highlight the Role of Bees in Urban Environments: Your materials should emphasize the critical role bees play in pollinating urban gardens, parks, and green spaces, contributing to biodiversity and local food production. Use compelling facts and figures to illustrate their impact, such as the variety of fruits and vegetables bees pollinate, which many urban residents enjoy.

Use Engaging Visuals: People are drawn to visually appealing content. Incorporate high-quality images of bees, hives, and urban gardens to make your materials more engaging. Visuals can also help explain complex concepts, like how pollination works or the structure of a bee colony, in an accessible way.

Create Diverse Content Formats: Diversify your educational materials to cater to different learning styles and preferences. Brochures and flyers are great for handouts during events or at local businesses. Online content, such as blog posts, infographics, and short videos, can reach a wider audience and is easily shared on social media. Consider creating interactive materials, like quizzes or games, especially for younger audiences to keep them engaged and interested in learning more about bees.

Incorporate Hands-On Learning Opportunities: Whenever possible, include information about local workshops, hive visits, or beekeeping classes in your materials. Hands-on experiences can significantly enhance learning and retention, providing a tangible connection to the subject matter.

Make It Action-Oriented: Encourage readers to take specific actions to support urban beekeeping and pollinator health. This could include planting bee-friendly flowers, avoiding pesticides, or even considering starting their own hive. Providing clear, simple steps individuals can take empowers them to contribute to bee conservation efforts.

Collaborate for Content Creation: Partner with local experts, educators, and environmental organizations to create your materials. These collaborations can enhance the quality and accuracy of your content and help distribute it through additional channels.

Accessibility Is Key: Ensure your materials are accessible to everyone, including those with disabilities. This means creating content that is easy to read, offering alternatives for visual elements (like alt text for images in online materials), and considering physical accessibility for in-person resources.

If you can create educational materials and resources that are informative, engaging, and accessible, you can play a crucial role in raising awareness about the importance of bees in urban environments. This not only supports bee conservation but also fosters a sense of community and shared responsibility for our urban ecosystems.

Public Demonstrations and Bee Safaris

One of the most engaging ways to captivate and educate urban audiences about the world of beekeeping is through public demonstrations and bee safaris. These interactive experiences offer a firsthand look at the inner workings of a bee colony and the day-to-day responsibilities of a beekeeper, effectively demystifying the process for those who may be unfamiliar or hesitant about the practice.

Organizing Bee Safaris and Public Hive Tours

Bee safaris and public hive tours require careful planning and organization to ensure they are both educational and safe for participants. Here are some steps and best practices to consider:

1. **Safety First:** Before organizing a public demonstration, ensure that all safety measures are in place. This includes having bee suits or veils for participants, preparing first-aid kits for potential stings, and ensuring that the demonstration area is secure and suitable for visitors of all ages.
2. **Educational Goals:** Define what you want participants to learn from the experience. Whether it's the importance of bees in our ecosystem, the basics of how a hive operates, or the process of honey production, having clear educational goals will help structure your demonstration and make it more impactful.
3. **Interactive Elements:** Incorporate interactive elements into your tour or demonstration. Allow participants to hold frames (under supervision), taste fresh honey directly from the hive, or even take part

in a mock beekeeping activity. Interactive elements make the experience memorable and engaging.

4. **Expert Guidance:** Ensure that knowledgeable beekeepers lead the safari or tour. Experts can provide accurate information, answer questions, and handle any unexpected situations that arise. Their passion and knowledge can greatly enhance the educational value of the demonstration.

5. **Pre-Visit Information:** Provide participants with pre-visit information. This could include what to expect during the tour, safety guidelines, what to wear, and why beekeeping is important. Educating participants before they arrive can enhance their understanding and enjoyment of the experience.

6. **Follow-Up Resources:** After the tour, offer resources for those interested in learning more or getting involved in beekeeping. This could be a list of recommended reading, links to beekeeping courses, or information about local beekeeping clubs.

Best Practices for Safe and Educational Demonstrations

- **Engage with Stories:** Use storytelling to share fascinating facts about bees and beekeeping. Personal anecdotes or surprising bee facts can capture the audience's attention and make the information more relatable.
- **Emphasize Conservation:** Highlight the role of bees in pollination and their importance to urban biodiversity. Discuss challenges bees face, such as habitat loss and pesticides, and how individuals can help.
- **Limit Group Sizes:** Keep groups small to ensure everyone can see, hear, and participate. Smaller groups are easier to manage and provide a more intimate learning experience.
- **Incorporate Technology:** Use technology, such as video or live feeds from inside the hive, to show aspects of bee life that might not be visible during the tour. This can provide a closer look at bee behavior and hive dynamics.

If you follow these guidelines, bee safaris and public demonstrations can become powerful tools for education and advocacy, inspiring a new generation of bee enthusiasts and environmental stewards in urban settings.

Collaboration with Local Businesses and Organizations

Partnering for Pollinator-Friendly Initiatives

In the heart of urban landscapes, where concrete often overshadows greenery, the importance of creating pollinator-friendly spaces cannot be overstated. Urban beekeepers have a unique role to play in this endeavor, serving not only as caretakers of their hives but also as advocates for broader ecological health. A key strategy in this advocacy is partnering with local businesses, parks, and community gardens to champion initiatives that support pollinators.

Local businesses, from cafes and restaurants to retail stores, often have spaces that can be transformed into havens for bees and other pollinators. Collaborating with these entities can lead to the establishment of rooftop gardens, the integration of pollinator-friendly plants in landscaping, and the adoption of pesticide-free practices. Such partnerships not only benefit the bees by providing essential foraging resources but also enhance the businesses' green credentials and appeal to environmentally conscious consumers.

Community gardens and city parks offer another avenue for collaboration. These green spaces are vital for urban biodiversity and can be optimized to better serve the needs of pollinators. Urban beekeepers can work with park managers and community garden organizers to introduce native flowering plants, establish bee hotels, and create educational signage to raise awareness about the importance of pollinators. These efforts contribute to a richer, more diverse urban ecosystem that supports the health and productivity of bee colonies.

Furthermore, engaging in these partnerships offers an opportunity to educate and involve the community in pollinator protection efforts. Workshops on creating pollinator-friendly gardens, talks on the importance of biodiversity, and hands-on activities such as building bee hotels can mobilize urban residents to take action. By fostering a sense of community ownership and responsibility for local ecosystems, urban beekeepers can inspire lasting change that extends far beyond their hives.

Collaboration with local businesses, parks, and community gardens to promote pollinator-friendly initiatives represents a powerful strategy for urban beekeepers to enhance the urban environment for bees. These partnerships not only provide critical resources for pollinators but also forge stronger connections between urban communities and the natural world. Through collective action, we can transform our cities into thriving ecosystems that support both people and pollinators.

Urban Beekeeping as a Business Booster

The appeal of local, sustainable products has never been higher among consumers. Urban beekeepers are in a prime position to capitalize on this trend by producing local honey, beeswax, and other bee-related products that resonate with consumers' desire for authenticity and environmental stewardship. Collaborating with local businesses offers a pathway to bring these products to market, while also raising awareness about the importance of bees in urban environments.

Benefits to Local Businesses

1. **Unique Selling Proposition**: For businesses, offering locally produced honey and bee-related products provides a unique selling proposition that can set them apart from competitors. It allows businesses to offer something truly local and sustainable, appealing to environmentally conscious consumers.
2. **Enhanced Brand Image**: Collaboration with urban beekeepers can enhance a business's brand image by associating it with sustainability, community support, and environmental stewardship. This positive brand image can attract more customers and improve customer loyalty.
3. **Educational Opportunities**: Partnering with urban beekeepers allows businesses to engage in educational outreach, informing customers

about the benefits of supporting local bees and the broader effects on urban biodiversity and food systems. This educational aspect can add value to the customer experience, turning a simple purchase into a learning opportunity.

Marketing Strategies

1. **Highlighting Locality and Sustainability**: Businesses should emphasize the local and sustainable aspects of their bee-related products in their marketing materials. This can include sharing the story of the urban beekeeper, the benefits of supporting local bees, and the environmental impact of urban beekeeping.
2. **Creating Experiences**: Offering beekeeping workshops, honey tastings, or tours of urban apiaries in collaboration with urban beekeepers can create unique experiences for customers, deepening their engagement with the brand and its values.
3. **Leveraging Social Media**: Using social media platforms to share stories, photos, and videos related to urban beekeeping and the production of bee-related products can engage a wider audience. Highlighting the collaboration between beekeepers and businesses through social media campaigns can raise awareness and drive interest.
4. **Partnership Branding**: Incorporating the branding of both the urban beekeeping initiative and the local business in product packaging and promotional materials can strengthen the partnership's visibility and appeal to consumers who value community collaboration.

Through thoughtful collaboration and targeted marketing strategies, urban beekeeping can provide significant benefits to local businesses, enhancing their product offerings and contributing to a positive community impact. By emphasizing the local, sustainable nature of their products and engaging customers in educational experiences, businesses can boost their brand image and support the vital role of bees in urban ecosystems.

Advocacy and Policy Influence

Urban beekeepers play a crucial role in advocating for policies and regulations that support bee-friendly environments and sustainable beekeeping practices within city landscapes. The urban beekeeping community, by virtue of its unique position at the intersection of agriculture, ecology, and urban living, has a powerful voice in shaping city policies towards more pollinator-friendly practices. Engaging in advocacy and policy influence is not only about ensuring the well-being of bees but also about contributing to the broader environmental sustainability goals of urban areas.

Engaging with City Officials and Decision-Makers

One of the most effective ways to advocate for bee-friendly policies is by engaging directly with city officials, planners, and decision-makers. Urban beekeepers can:

- **Identify Key Stakeholders:** Research and identify city council members, environmental committees, and local planning departments responsible for urban agriculture, parks, and green spaces.
- **Prepare Your Case:** Arm yourself with data and research on the benefits of urban beekeeping, including pollination benefits, biodiversity enhancement, and community well-being.
- **Schedule Meetings:** Request meetings with stakeholders to discuss the importance of bee-friendly policies, presenting your case in a concise and compelling manner.

Participating in Community Planning Meetings

Community planning meetings offer a platform for public input into local policies, urban development plans, and environmental initiatives. Urban beekeepers can leverage these meetings to:

- **Voice Concerns:** Use these forums to express the need for integrating bee-friendly initiatives into urban planning, such as planting pollinator gardens in public parks or establishing beekeeping zones.

- **Submit Proposals:** Prepare and submit proposals for bee-friendly projects, highlighting their benefits to the community and environment.
- **Build Alliances:** Collaborate with other environmental and community groups to strengthen your advocacy efforts, creating a unified front that is harder for officials to ignore.

Tips for Effective Advocacy

- **Stay Informed:** Keep abreast of local government agendas, meetings, and planning sessions where issues affecting bees and beekeeping might be discussed.
- **Be Professional:** Present your arguments logically and professionally, backed by evidence and examples of successful urban beekeeping models.
- **Utilize Social Media and Press:** Use social media platforms and local press to raise awareness and garner public support for bee-friendly policies.
- **Offer Solutions:** Instead of merely highlighting problems, propose practical, achievable solutions that city officials can implement.
- **Foster Relationships:** Develop ongoing relationships with city officials and staff, becoming a go-to resource for issues related to bees and pollination in the urban context.

Through advocacy and active participation in policymaking, urban beekeepers can significantly influence the creation of a more inclusive, sustainable, and bee-friendly urban environment. This not only benefits the bees and the immediate beekeeping community, but also enhances the overall ecological health and livability of cities.

Conclusion

Engaging with the community and collaborating with local businesses and organizations are fundamental aspects of successful urban beekeeping. Through educational outreach, we have the power to transform public perception and foster a deep appreciation for bees and their critical role in our ecosystems. By building partnerships and advocating for bee-friendly policies, urban beekeepers can create a supportive environment that benefits both bees and people. This chapter has equipped you with strategies to connect, educate, and advocate effectively, laying the groundwork for a thriving urban beekeeping community. As we move forward, remember that each interaction, no matter how small, contributes to a larger movement towards sustainability and ecological health in our urban landscapes. Let's continue to work together, leveraging our collective efforts to ensure a bright future for urban beekeeping and the precious pollinators we aim to protect.

Chapter 9: Overcoming Challenges in Urban Beekeeping

Urban beekeeping embodies the remarkable resilience and adaptability of both bees and their keepers, flourishing within the heart of bustling cities. However, this unique environment presents a distinct set of challenges that can test the resolve and resourcefulness of even the most experienced beekeepers. From navigating the complexities of pests, diseases, and predators in densely populated areas to addressing public concerns and ensuring the security of hives against theft and vandalism, the urban beekeeper's journey is fraught with obstacles.

This chapter aims to shed light on these challenges, offering practical strategies and solutions to mitigate them. Through understanding, preparation, and community engagement, urban beekeepers can overcome these hurdles, ensuring the health and prosperity of their colonies while fostering a positive relationship with the urban ecosystem around them. With the right approach, the challenges of urban beekeeping can be transformed into opportunities for growth, education, and advocacy, contributing to a richer, more sustainable urban life.

Security Measures for Urban Hives

Preventing Hive Theft and Vandalism

Urban beekeeping, while rewarding, introduces unique security concerns not typically faced by rural beekeepers. In the city, hives are more susceptible to theft and vandalism, given their proximity to large populations and the ease of access for potential perpetrators. Protecting these vital pollinators requires thoughtful strategies to deter unauthorized access and minimize risks. Here, we outline practical measures to safeguard urban hives, ensuring they remain secure and productive.

Location Choices

The first line of defense in protecting urban hives is selecting an optimal location. A well-chosen site is not only crucial for the bees' health and productivity but also for their security. Consider placing hives in less visible and hard-to-reach areas without compromising the bees' flight paths or access to forage. Rooftops of buildings offer an excellent option, as they are typically inaccessible to the general public and provide a secluded environment for the bees. Balconies and enclosed gardens can also serve as secure locations, provided they are not easily visible or accessible from the street.

Locks and Hive Anchoring Techniques

Securing hives physically can deter theft and reduce the risk of vandalism. Using locks and hive straps ensures that hives cannot be easily opened or removed. Hive stands with locking mechanisms can be employed to anchor hives to their location, making it difficult for them to be carried away. For added security, consider using chains and padlocks to attach hives to immovable objects. It's important, however, to ensure that any security measures do not obstruct hive ventilation or the bees' entrance and exit paths.

Camouflage and Strategic Placement

Camouflaging hives can effectively reduce their visibility, making them less likely to be targeted by vandals or thieves. Painting hives in colors that blend with the surroundings or using natural barriers like bushes and trees can help hide hives from unwanted attention. Additionally, strategic placement of hives within the landscape, such as behind structures or within secluded parts of a garden, can further obscure them from view.

Community Engagement

Engaging with the local community can be one of the most effective strategies for protecting urban hives. By educating neighbors and local residents about the importance of bees and the specifics of your beekeeping activities, you can foster a supportive environment. Informed community members are more likely to respect your beekeeping efforts and can serve as additional eyes and ears, helping to monitor the hives for suspicious activity. Establishing a good relationship with neighbors may also encourage them to report any vandalism or theft attempts to you or the authorities.

Implementing these security measures requires a balance between accessibility for the beekeeper and deterrence against potential threats. By carefully considering hive placement, employing physical security measures, camouflaging hives, and engaging with the community, urban beekeepers can significantly reduce the risk of theft and vandalism, ensuring a safe and productive environment for their colonies.

Technology and Hive Security

In the dynamic environment of urban beekeeping, safeguarding hives against theft and vandalism is a paramount concern. Fortunately, advancements in technology provide a robust toolkit for beekeepers to enhance the security of their urban hives. This section explores innovative technological solutions and community-based strategies to protect urban bee colonies, ensuring their safety and thriving existence amidst city life.

Utilizing Technology for Hive Security

- **GPS Trackers:** Embedding GPS trackers within hives offers a discreet yet powerful way to monitor their location. In the event of theft, these devices enable beekeepers to track and recover their hives promptly. GPS tracking not only acts as a deterrent to potential thieves but also provides peace of mind to the beekeeper, knowing their hives can be traced.
- **Motion Sensors and Alarms:** Installing motion sensors around hives can alert beekeepers to unauthorized access or tampering. These sensors can be connected to alarms that either emit loud sounds to scare off intruders or send alerts directly to the beekeeper's phone. Some advanced systems allow for sensitivity

adjustments to prevent false alarms caused by the bees themselves or small animals.

- **Surveillance Cameras:** Surveillance cameras serve multiple purposes; they can deter potential vandals or thieves, document unauthorized activities, and provide real-time monitoring of the hives. Cameras with night vision capabilities ensure round-the-clock surveillance, while motion-activated recording can conserve storage and focus attention on periods of activity.

The Role of Community Watch Programs and Local Law Enforcement

- **Community Watch Programs:** Engaging with neighborhood watch or community watch programs can be incredibly effective in enhancing hive security. Informing neighbors about the presence of your hives and their importance to urban biodiversity can enlist their support in keeping an eye out for suspicious activities. A community that values its local beekeeping efforts is more likely to report theft or vandalism, acting as an extended network of guardians.
- **Collaboration with Local Law Enforcement:** Establishing a relationship with local law enforcement agencies can significantly enhance the security measures in place. By informing local police about your beekeeping activities, you can ensure a quicker and more informed response in case of theft or vandalism. Law enforcement officers can also provide valuable advice on securing your hives and may offer to include your beekeeping location in their regular patrol routes, adding an extra layer of security.

Integrating technology with community-based security efforts offers a comprehensive approach to protecting urban hives. These strategies not only safeguard the physical hives but also promote a culture of respect and appreciation for urban beekeeping within the community. By adopting these measures, urban beekeepers can focus more on the joys and rewards of their practice, secure in the knowledge that their hives are well-protected.

Managing Public Concerns and Safety

Addressing Fears and Allergies

Urban beekeeping requires not only the care and management of bee colonies but also diligent attention to public concerns and safety, particularly regarding fears and allergies. Effective communication and education play pivotal roles in fostering a harmonious relationship between urban beekeepers, their neighbors, and the wider community.

Effective Communication Strategies to Alleviate Public Fears about Bees

- **Educational Outreach**: One of the most effective ways to alleviate fears is through education. Offering informational sessions, workshops, or open house days at your beekeeping site can help demystify bees and their behavior. Highlight the importance of bees in pollination and their role in the urban ecosystem.
- **Transparent Communication**: Keep neighbors informed about your beekeeping activities and the measures you're taking to ensure public safety. Regular updates can build trust and reduce fear.
- **Bee Behavior Education**: Many people confuse bees with wasps and other more aggressive insects. Educate your community on the generally docile nature of honeybees and their tendency to sting only when provoked or defending their hive.
- **Success Stories**: Share positive stories and experiences from urban beekeeping, including benefits such as increased pollination, biodiversity, and local honey production. Success stories can help change perceptions and build community support.

Creating a Plan for Dealing with Potential Allergic Reactions

- **Allergy Awareness**: It's crucial to acknowledge and plan for the possibility of allergic reactions within the community. Engage with local health professionals to provide information and training on recognizing and responding to bee sting allergies.

- **Emergency Action Plan**: Develop a clear, concise action plan for bee sting incidents, including emergency contact information, location of first aid kits with epinephrine auto-injectors (if available), and instructions for their use. Make sure this plan is well communicated to your neighbors and local health services.
- **Educational Materials on Bee Allergies**: Distribute materials that educate the community on bee sting allergies, symptoms to watch for, and when to seek medical attention. This information can help demystify allergic reactions and provide practical advice for handling them.
- **Collaboration with Health Services**: Partner with local health clinics, hospitals, and allergy specialists to offer informational sessions on bee sting prevention and treatment. Collaborative efforts can enhance community trust and safety.

If you implement these strategies, you can significantly reduce public fears and concerns about bees, fostering a safer and more informed community. Education and communication are key to transforming apprehension into appreciation, enabling urban beekeepers to practice their craft with broader community support and understanding.

Creating a Bee-Safe Environment

Designing Hive Setups to Minimize Human-Bee Interactions

One of the primary concerns in urban beekeeping is ensuring that bee activity does not adversely affect the surrounding human population. Thoughtful placement and design of hive setups are crucial in achieving this goal. By considering the flight paths of bees and incorporating barrier plantings, beekeepers can significantly reduce the chances of bees and humans crossing paths.

- **Flight Path Considerations:** Bees typically fly straight out of their hive entrance when they begin their foraging expeditions. Understanding this behavior allows urban beekeepers to strategically place hives so that the bees' flight paths are directed away from pedestrian areas and communal spaces. Elevating hives on rooftops or positioning them to face towards gardens or parks can help direct bees into less populated areas, minimizing interactions with humans.

- **Barrier Plantings:** Planting tall, dense vegetation or constructing physical barriers around hives can help guide bees to fly at higher altitudes over people's heads, reducing the likelihood of encounters. Suitable barrier plants include tall shrubs, hedges, or even trellises with climbing plants. These not only serve to redirect the bees' flight paths but also enhance the aesthetic appeal of the beekeeping setup and contribute additional foraging resources for the bees.

Implementing Best Practices for Bee Behavior Management

Managing bee behavior is another vital aspect of creating a bee-safe environment in urban areas. By understanding and influencing how bees behave, beekeepers can prevent swarming and reduce aggressive behavior, which are common concerns among the public.

- **Swarm Management:** Swarming is a natural part of a bee colony's reproductive cycle but can be alarming to the public. Regular hive inspections can help beekeepers identify signs of impending swarming, such as the construction of queen cells. Techniques such as splitting hives, requeening, or providing additional space and resources can help prevent swarms from occurring. Educating the public about swarming behavior and having a swarm capture plan in place can also mitigate concerns.
- **Reducing Aggressive Behavior:** Bee aggression can often be mitigated by selecting bee strains known for their gentle nature. Regularly replacing queens with those from reputable sources that breed for docility can help maintain a calm colony. Additionally, beekeepers should avoid working with hives during peak pedestrian times or in adverse weather conditions, which can increase bee irritability. Providing adequate water sources near the hive can also prevent bees from seeking water in neighboring areas, further reducing the chance of human-bee interactions.

These strategies mean urban beekeepers can create a safe and harmonious environment for both bees and the surrounding community. These practices not only contribute to the success and sustainability of urban beekeeping but also help in fostering a positive perception of bees among city dwellers, promoting coexistence and understanding.

Emergency Response Plans

Developing and Communicating a Clear Plan for Responding to Bee-Related Incidents

The foundation of urban beekeeping success lies not only in the health and productivity of the bee colonies but also in the beekeeper's preparedness to handle unexpected incidents involving their bees. A crucial aspect of this preparedness is the development and communication of an emergency response plan tailored to bee-related incidents. This plan should outline specific steps to be taken in the event of a bee swarm, bee attack, or an individual being stung, particularly if they are allergic.

Key elements of an effective emergency response plan include:

- **Immediate Steps for Bee Stings:** Instructions on how to safely remove a bee sting, apply first aid, and recognize signs of an allergic reaction.
- **Contact Information:** A list of emergency contacts, including local health services, poison control centers, and emergency responders who are aware of and prepared for potential bee-related emergencies.
- **Communication Protocol:** Guidelines on how to quickly inform neighbors, local schools, and businesses about an ongoing incident, utilizing community networks, social media, or direct communication methods.
- **Swarm Management:** Strategies for safely capturing and relocating a swarm that has left the hive, including the role of the beekeeper and when to call a professional bee remover.

©Anthony Carter | www.beekeeping-101.com |part of Carman Online Content Publishing Ltd

Collaboration with Local Health and Emergency Services for Rapid Response to Allergic Reactions or Other Bee-Related Emergencies

Collaboration with local health and emergency services is paramount to ensure a rapid and effective response to bee-related emergencies, especially those involving allergic reactions. By establishing a relationship with these services in advance, urban beekeepers can help ensure that first responders are prepared with the appropriate knowledge and equipment to deal with bee stings and potential allergic reactions.

Steps to foster effective collaboration include:

- **Educational Outreach:** Providing local health and emergency services with information on bees, bee behavior, and the specifics of bee sting treatment and allergic reaction management.
- **Workshops and Training:** Organizing or participating in workshops and training sessions for emergency responders and health professionals on the proper response to bee-related incidents.
- **Shared Response Plan:** Developing a shared emergency response plan that includes protocols for communication and action between the beekeeper, emergency services, and the community.
- **Regular Updates:** Keeping local health and emergency services updated on the status of your beekeeping activities, including any changes in hive locations or the number of hives being managed.

If you employ these strategies, you can create a safer environment for your bees, yourself, and your community. An effective emergency response plan, combined with strong collaboration with local health and emergency services, lays the foundation for a proactive approach to managing public concerns and safety in urban beekeeping.

©Anthony Carter | www.beekeeping-101.com |part of Carman Online Content Publishing Ltd

Innovative Solutions to Urban Beekeeping Challenges

Urban Beekeeping Collaboratives

One of the most effective strategies for overcoming the unique challenges of urban beekeeping is through the formation or participation in beekeeping collaboratives and networks. These groups offer a platform for urban beekeepers to pool resources, share knowledge, and provide mutual support, creating a community that is well-equipped to tackle the hurdles of beekeeping in a city environment.

The Power of Collaboration

Urban beekeeping collaboratives bring together individuals who share a common interest in beekeeping within city limits. These groups often range from hobbyists with a single hive to more experienced beekeepers managing several colonies. By uniting, members can leverage collective knowledge and experiences, leading to innovative solutions that might be difficult to achieve independently.

Shared Resources and Economies of Scale

One of the primary benefits of beekeeping collaboratives is the ability to share resources. This can include the collective purchasing of beekeeping supplies, which can reduce costs through bulk buying. Equipment that might be too expensive for an individual beekeeper, such as honey extractors or specialized tools, can be purchased collectively and shared among members. Additionally, these networks can facilitate the sharing of physical spaces for beekeeping activities, crucial in urban areas where space is a premium.

Knowledge Exchange and Education

Beekeeping collaboratives serve as a hub for education and knowledge exchange. They organize workshops, training sessions, and mentorship programs for both novice and experienced beekeepers. This continuous learning environment helps urban beekeepers stay updated on best practices, pest management techniques, and innovative hive designs suited for urban settings. Through regular meetings and forums, members can discuss challenges, share successes, and collectively troubleshoot problems.

Mutual Support and Problem-Solving

Urban beekeeping presents a unique set of challenges, from navigating local regulations to managing hives in limited spaces. Collaboratives offer a support network where beekeepers can seek advice and assistance from peers who understand the intricacies of urban beekeeping. This mutual support extends to collective problem-solving, where members can come together to address issues such as pest outbreaks, disease management, and community concerns about bees.

Enhancing Community Engagement

Beyond the immediate benefits to beekeepers, collaboratives play a vital role in engaging and educating the broader community about the importance of bees in urban environments. They can lead initiatives to create bee-friendly spaces, partner with local schools and organizations for educational programs, and advocate for policies that support urban beekeeping. Through these efforts, beekeeping collaboratives help to foster a positive relationship between urban beekeepers and the wider community, highlighting the essential role bees play in sustaining urban ecosystems.

Urban beekeeping collaboratives and networks embody the spirit of community and cooperation. By joining forces, urban beekeepers can overcome the challenges of their unique environment, enhance their beekeeping practices, and make a positive impact on their local communities and urban biodiversity as a whole.

Advocacy and Policy Engagement

Engagement with local governments and organizations plays a pivotal role in shaping a supportive environment for urban beekeeping. By advocating for bee-friendly policies and urban planning, beekeepers can contribute to the development of cities that not only accommodate but also support and thrive on the presence of bees. Here's how urban beekeepers can navigate and contribute to this process:

Understanding Local Policy Frameworks

- Familiarize yourself with current city policies, zoning laws, and regulations related to beekeeping. This knowledge forms the basis for informed advocacy and engagement.
- Identify gaps or restrictive policies in the current urban planning frameworks that limit the potential for urban beekeeping.

Building Relationships with Local Governments and Organizations

- Establish connections with local government officials, urban planners, and environmental organizations. Regular communication and building a network of allies can significantly enhance the effectiveness of advocacy efforts.
- Participate in public meetings, workshops, and forums related to urban development and environmental sustainability to raise awareness of the importance of urban beekeeping.

Presenting the Case for Bee-Friendly Urban Environments

- Develop a compelling argument for the inclusion of bee-friendly initiatives in urban planning, highlighting the benefits such as enhanced biodiversity, improved pollination rates, and the promotion of green spaces.
- Provide evidence-based proposals that demonstrate the positive impact of urban beekeeping on local ecosystems and communities.

This could include case studies, research findings, and testimonials from successful urban beekeeping projects.

Lobbying for Policy Changes and Initiatives

- Work collaboratively with environmental groups and beekeeping associations to lobby for changes in local policies that support urban beekeeping. This could involve proposing specific amendments to zoning laws, advocating for the creation of pollinator-friendly spaces, or seeking funding for urban beekeeping education and outreach programs.
- Propose the integration of beekeeping considerations into broader urban sustainability and green space initiatives, ensuring that the needs of urban bee populations are considered in city planning decisions.

Promoting Urban Sustainability Initiatives

- Actively participate in and support urban sustainability initiatives that benefit not only bees but also the wider environment. This includes initiatives focused on increasing green spaces, planting native flowers and plants, and reducing pesticide use.
- By highlighting the role of bees in achieving urban sustainability goals, beekeepers can encourage a more inclusive approach to city planning that recognizes the value of biodiversity and ecosystem services.

Educational Outreach and Community Engagement

- Educate policymakers, community leaders, and the public about the benefits of urban beekeeping through workshops, seminars, and informational campaigns. Increasing awareness and understanding can help garner support for bee-friendly policies.
- Engage the community in discussions about urban beekeeping, inviting input and collaboration. This inclusive approach can help dispel myths and build a strong foundation of support for beekeeping initiatives.

Advocacy and policy engagement are critical for creating an urban landscape that supports beekeeping and promotes ecological health. By taking an active role in these efforts, urban beekeepers can help shape cities that not only tolerate but actively embrace and benefit from the presence of bees, setting a precedent for sustainable urban living.

©Anthony Carter | www.beekeeping-101.com |part of Carman Online Content Publishing Ltd

Chapter 10: Future of Urban Beekeeping

As we venture into the concluding chapter of our guide, "Urban Beekeeping: Managing Hives in City Environments," we turn our gaze towards the horizon, exploring the promising future that urban beekeeping holds. This chapter is not just a culmination of practical insights and experiences shared throughout the book but a forward-looking vision that anticipates the evolution of beekeeping in urban landscapes. With cities growing and green spaces becoming ever more vital, the importance of urban beekeeping in promoting biodiversity, enhancing community bonds, and advancing sustainable practices has never been more pronounced. Here, we delve into the technological innovations that are redefining how we interact with and care for our urban bee colonies, the expanding community of urban beekeepers who are making this practice more inclusive and widespread, and the sustainable approaches that promise a greener, more resilient urban future. This chapter aims to inspire, educate, and challenge us to think about the role urban beekeeping will play in the cities of tomorrow, highlighting the potential for positive impact on our communities, our environment, and the world at large.

Technological Advances in Beekeeping

Monitoring and Management Tools

Smart Hive Technology

In the realm of urban beekeeping, technological innovation plays a pivotal role in transforming how we manage and interact with our hives. Smart hive technology, powered by the Internet of Things (IoT), stands at the forefront of this transformation, offering beekeepers unprecedented insights into the health and behavior of their colonies. These advanced systems integrate sensors within the hive to monitor a range of critical parameters, including temperature, humidity, bee activity, and even hive weight, which can indicate honey production levels.

The integration of IoT devices into beekeeping practices enables beekeepers to remotely monitor the condition of their hives in real-time, receiving alerts on their smartphones or computers when the data indicates potential issues. This capability is especially valuable in urban environments, where space constraints and the proximity of hives to human activity necessitate careful management to ensure both bee and public safety.

Smart hive technology not only simplifies hive management but also enhances the beekeeper's ability to make informed decisions. For instance, sudden drops in temperature within the hive can prompt beekeepers to take measures to insulate their hives against cold weather, while unusual patterns in bee activity may indicate health issues or the onset of swarming behavior. By providing timely data, these tools allow for proactive management, reducing the risk of colony loss and improving overall hive health.

Data-Driven Beekeeping

The advent of data-driven beekeeping marks a significant shift towards more scientific and informed approaches to managing bee colonies. By collecting and analyzing data from urban hives, beekeepers can gain a deeper understanding of bee health, behaviors, and the effects of urban environments on pollinator activity. This wealth of data not only benefits individual beekeepers but also contributes to broader research efforts aimed at improving urban beekeeping practices and pollinator conservation.

Several platforms and apps have emerged to facilitate the sharing and analysis of beekeeping data among the community. These tools offer features such as data logging, visual analytics, and community forums where beekeepers can compare notes, identify patterns, and share best practices. For example, an app might analyze data collected from a network of smart hives across a city, identifying which areas provide the best forage for bees based on hive weight gain or activity levels. This information can guide urban planning and community planting initiatives, ensuring that cities are landscaped in ways that support pollinator health and biodiversity.

Moreover, data-driven beekeeping opens the door to citizen science, where urban beekeepers contribute to large-scale studies on bee health and urban ecology. By pooling data from numerous hives, researchers can identify trends, track the spread of diseases, and evaluate the impact of environmental changes on bee populations. This collaborative approach not only enriches our understanding of bees and their role in urban ecosystems but also empowers beekeepers to be part of the solution to challenges facing pollinators today.

In embracing these technological advancements, urban beekeepers are equipped with the tools and knowledge necessary to ensure the prosperity of their hives and the sustainability of urban beekeeping. As we continue to innovate, the future of urban beekeeping looks brighter, smarter, and more connected than ever before.

Innovative Hive Designs

As urban beekeeping continues to gain popularity, the demand for hive designs that not only suit the practical needs of bees but also the spatial and aesthetic requirements of urban environments has led to remarkable innovations. These innovative hive designs are at the forefront of making beekeeping more accessible, enjoyable, and harmoniously integrated into cityscapes.

Modular Hive Systems

Modular hive systems represent a significant advancement in urban beekeeping, offering flexibility and scalability that traditional hives cannot match. These systems allow beekeepers to easily adjust hive size and configuration to accommodate colony growth or shrinkage, and to manage their bees more effectively within limited spaces. The modular design also facilitates easier hive inspections and management tasks, reducing the stress on both bees and beekeepers. Moreover, their sleek and modern aesthetics can blend seamlessly with urban architecture, making them an attractive addition to rooftops, balconies, and gardens.

Space-Saving Hives

Space-saving hives, such as vertical or stackable models, are designed to maximize beekeeping potential in confined areas. These hives take advantage of vertical space, which is often under-utilized in urban settings, allowing for the expansion of bee colonies without requiring additional ground space. This design is particularly beneficial for rooftop and balcony beekeepers who face limitations on footprint. Additionally, space-saving hives can be designed with integrated features such as built-in feeders and water sources, enhancing the efficiency of hive management.

Aesthetically Pleasing Models

The importance of aesthetics in hive design cannot be overstated, especially in urban environments where the appearance of beekeeping setups can influence public perception and acceptance. Hives are now being designed with a range of materials, colors, and finishes that not only withstand the elements but also complement urban aesthetics. From wooden hives that offer a natural, rustic look to sleek, modern designs that reflect contemporary architectural styles, the options available enable beekeepers to choose hives that reflect their personal taste and blend with their surroundings.

Integration into Urban Landscapes

The integration of innovative hive designs into urban landscapes goes beyond aesthetics and space efficiency. These designs often incorporate features that address urban-specific challenges, such as improved ventilation systems for heat management in densely built-up areas, and secure mounting systems to protect hives from high winds on rooftops. Some designs also focus on promoting bee health and safety, with features that deter pests and predators common in urban areas.

Making Beekeeping More Accessible and Enjoyable

The development of innovative hive designs plays a crucial role in making beekeeping more accessible to a wider audience. By addressing the unique challenges of urban environments, these designs lower the barriers to entry for new beekeepers and enhance the experience for seasoned practitioners. They make the practice of beekeeping not just a possibility but a pleasure in urban settings, encouraging more individuals to embark on the rewarding journey of beekeeping.

In conclusion, the evolution of hive designs is a testament to the ingenuity and creativity of the beekeeping community. As these designs continue to evolve, they will undoubtedly play a pivotal role in the future of urban beekeeping, making it easier, more productive, and more enjoyable for beekeepers and their bees alike.

Expanding the Urban Beekeeping Community

Initiatives for Inclusive Beekeeping

At the heart of the urban beekeeping revolution lies a commitment not only to the bees but also to the communities that surround them. As the practice of beekeeping in city environments continues to flourish, a crucial aspect of its evolution is ensuring it becomes an inclusive endeavor. A diverse beekeeping community strengthens our collective understanding and appreciation of bees, enriching the urban beekeeping experience for everyone involved. This section explores the various initiatives and programs designed to foster inclusivity within the urban beekeeping community, reaching out to schools, underserved communities, and emphasizing the creation of inclusive spaces for learning and engagement.

Bridging the Gap through Education

Education serves as a powerful tool in demystifying beekeeping and making it accessible to a broader audience. Innovative programs aimed at schools introduce young minds to the importance of bees in our ecosystem, sparking early interest in beekeeping as a hobby or career path. These initiatives often incorporate hands-on learning experiences, such as school garden projects and observation hives, allowing students to witness the fascinating world of bees up close. By embedding beekeeping education within the curriculum, we not only educate the next generation on the significance of pollinators, but also encourage stewardship of our environment from a young age.

Reaching Underserved Communities

Urban beekeeping initiatives increasingly recognize the importance of engaging underserved communities, often marginalized in environmental and sustainability conversations. Collaborations between beekeeping organizations and community groups lead to the establishment of community hives, beekeeping scholarships, and training programs tailored to these communities. Such efforts aim to empower individuals with the knowledge and skills to participate in beekeeping, fostering economic opportunities and enhancing community green spaces. By breaking down barriers to entry, these initiatives ensure that beekeeping is seen as a viable and rewarding pursuit for all, regardless of socioeconomic background.

Creating Inclusive Spaces for Engagement

The essence of inclusivity in urban beekeeping also lies in creating spaces where individuals from all walks of life feel welcome to learn, share, and connect over beekeeping. Community gardens, urban farms, and beekeeping co-ops serve as communal hubs for beekeeping activities, offering workshops, mentorship programs, and events that cater to diverse interests and skill levels. These spaces not only provide practical beekeeping resources but also foster a sense of belonging and community among urban beekeepers. They become venues for cross-cultural exchange and learning, enriching the urban beekeeping community with a tapestry of perspectives and experiences.

Supporting Inclusivity through Policy and Advocacy

Advocacy plays a crucial role in promoting inclusivity within urban beekeeping. By advocating for policies that support urban agriculture and beekeeping, beekeeping organizations and community leaders can influence the creation of more inclusive and supportive environments for urban beekeepers. This includes pushing for accessible green spaces, bee-friendly planting policies in public areas, and financial support for beekeeping initiatives targeting underserved populations. Through these efforts, the urban beekeeping community can grow not just in numbers but in diversity and strength, reflecting the vibrant mosaic of the cities they inhabit.

Conclusion

The future of urban beekeeping is intrinsically linked to its ability to be inclusive and accessible to all. By embracing initiatives that reach out to schools, underserved communities, and by creating inclusive spaces for learning and engagement, we not only enrich the urban beekeeping community but also ensure its sustainability and relevance in the urban landscapes of tomorrow. These efforts highlight the transformative power of beekeeping to bring communities together, fostering a shared commitment to environmental stewardship and the wellbeing of our urban ecosystems.

Advocacy for Urban Beekeeping Policies

Urban beekeepers play a pivotal role in shaping the policies that govern our cities, turning urban environments into thriving habitats for bees and other pollinators. Through advocacy and engagement, beekeepers have the power to influence local regulations, transforming urban landscapes into more bee-friendly spaces. This section explores the impact of advocacy on urban beekeeping policies, offering examples of successful efforts that have led to significant changes in local regulations, public space management, and community gardening practices.

The Power of Beekeeper Advocacy

Beekeepers, by virtue of their passion and knowledge about pollinators, are uniquely positioned to advocate for changes that not only benefit bees but also the broader urban ecosystem. Engaging with city officials, taking part in local environmental committees, and collaborating with urban planning departments are just some of the ways beekeepers have successfully raised awareness about the importance of bee-friendly policies. These advocacy efforts often focus on the critical role bees play in urban agriculture, biodiversity, and the overall health of urban green spaces.

Successful Advocacy Efforts

- **Revision of Local Zoning Laws**: In many cities, beekeepers have successfully lobbied for the revision of zoning laws that previously restricted beekeeping activities. By presenting well-researched arguments highlighting the benefits of urban beekeeping, along with proposed guidelines to ensure public safety and hive health, beekeepers have persuaded city councils to adopt more favorable regulations.
- **Creation of Pollinator-Friendly Spaces**: Beekeepers have played a crucial role in the establishment of pollinator-friendly spaces within urban areas. Through partnerships with city parks departments and community organizations, beekeepers have helped to design and implement pollinator gardens in public parks, schoolyards, and along city streets. These gardens not only provide essential forage for bees but also serve as educational tools to engage the community about the importance of pollinators.
- **Adoption of Pesticide Regulations**: Recognizing the harmful impact of certain pesticides on bee populations, urban beekeepers have advocated for the adoption of city-wide pesticide management policies that favor the use of bee-friendly alternatives. These efforts often involve educating policymakers and the public about the risks associated with pesticide use and presenting evidence-based recommendations for safer pest management practices.

Impact of Advocacy on Urban Beekeeping

The impact of advocacy by urban beekeepers extends far beyond the hives. Successful advocacy efforts have led to a greater recognition of the value of bees in urban environments, encouraging cities to integrate pollinator health into their sustainability and biodiversity strategies. Moreover, these efforts have fostered a sense of community among urban beekeepers, environmentalists, gardeners, and city residents, creating a collective movement towards more sustainable and pollinator-friendly urban landscapes.

Moving Forward

As urban beekeeping continues to gain momentum, the role of beekeeper advocacy in shaping supportive city policies becomes increasingly important. By continuing to engage with policymakers, collaborating with like-minded organizations, and educating the public about the benefits of urban beekeeping, beekeepers can ensure that cities become ever more welcoming places for bees and other pollinators. This collective endeavor not only enriches our urban ecosystems but also strengthens the bond between urban communities and the natural world, paving the way for a more sustainable and interconnected future.

Building Networks and Collaborations

In the journey to expand the urban beekeeping community, the creation and nurturing of both local and global networks stand as pillars for sharing knowledge, resources, and support among urban beekeepers. These networks not only serve as conduits for the exchange of invaluable insights and experiences but also foster a sense of camaraderie and collective purpose. Collaborations with environmental organizations, academic institutions, and local governments further amplify the positive impact of urban beekeeping on biodiversity and community well-being.

Local Networks: Strengthening Community Ties

Local beekeeping associations and clubs play a crucial role in bringing urban beekeepers together, offering a platform for education, mentorship, and support. These organizations often host workshops, seminars, and social events that enable beekeepers to learn from each other, share challenges and successes, and stay updated on best practices and local regulations. By fostering a tight-knit community, these networks ensure that both novice and experienced beekeepers have access to the resources and encouragement needed to thrive in urban environments.

Global Networks: Sharing and Learning Without Borders

The digital age has facilitated the creation of global networks where urban beekeepers from different parts of the world can connect. Online forums, social media groups, and beekeeping websites offer spaces for beekeepers to exchange knowledge, discuss challenges unique to urban settings, and share innovative solutions. These global connections not only enrich the urban beekeeping experience but also highlight the universal importance of beekeeping in promoting environmental stewardship and sustainability.

Collaborations with Environmental Organizations and Academic Institutions

Partnerships with environmental organizations and academic institutions can significantly enhance the scope and impact of urban beekeeping initiatives. These collaborations can lead to research projects that investigate the effects of urban beekeeping on local ecosystems, pollinator health, and urban agriculture. They also provide opportunities for educational outreach, raising awareness about the importance of bees and pollinators among the general public and fostering a culture of conservation and environmental responsibility.

Engaging with Local Governments

Engagement with local governments is essential for the development of supportive policies and programs that facilitate urban beekeeping.

Beekeepers and beekeeping associations can advocate for the inclusion of bee-friendly practices in urban planning, such as the creation of pollinator pathways and the reduction of pesticide use in public spaces. By demonstrating the benefits of urban beekeeping, such as enhanced pollination services and increased urban greenery, beekeepers can influence policy changes that support biodiversity and improve the quality of life in urban areas.

The Ripple Effect of Networks and Collaborations

The networks and collaborations formed within the urban beekeeping community have a ripple effect, extending beyond individual beekeepers and hives to touch entire communities and ecosystems. Through shared efforts and collective action, urban beekeepers can contribute to a more sustainable, resilient, and interconnected urban future. By building bridges between individuals, organizations, and governments, the urban beekeeping community can drive positive change, ensuring that cities not only accommodate but also thrive with the presence of bees and other pollinators.

Sustainable Urban Beekeeping

Promoting Urban Biodiversity

As urban areas continue to expand, the importance of creating and maintaining biodiverse green spaces has become increasingly crucial for the health of our planet and the wellbeing of its inhabitants, including humans and pollinators alike. Urban beekeepers play a pivotal role in this endeavor, serving as advocates for and practitioners of biodiversity through the promotion of pollinator-friendly environments. This section outlines strategies for enhancing urban biodiversity, focusing on the support of bee populations and other pollinators through thoughtful planting, pesticide management, and the development of green corridors.

Pollinator-Friendly Planting

Urban beekeepers can lead by example, transforming their own spaces, however small, into rich sources of nourishment for bees and other pollinators. This involves selecting a variety of native plants that flower at different times of the year, ensuring a consistent supply of food. Planting in clusters can also make it easier for bees to locate and gather nectar and pollen. Beyond personal gardens, beekeepers can engage with community gardens, schools, and public parks, encouraging the adoption of pollinator-friendly plants.

Key considerations for pollinator-friendly planting include:

- **Diversity**: Choose a wide range of plants that bloom from early spring to late fall.
- **Native species**: Favor native plants that are well adapted to the local climate and soil, requiring less water and maintenance, and providing the best resources for local wildlife.
- **Avoiding double flowers**: Go for single-flower tops (e.g., daisies and marigolds) over double flower tops, as they offer easier access to pollen and nectar.

Pesticide Reduction

Pesticides pose a significant threat to bees and other pollinators by contaminating their food sources and habitats. Urban beekeepers can advocate for and practice integrated pest management techniques that minimize the use of chemicals, favoring natural predators and biological controls. Educating the community about the harmful effects of pesticides and promoting organic gardening practices can help reduce the use of these chemicals in urban areas.

Strategies include:

- **Education**: Host workshops or create informational materials on organic gardening and natural pest control methods.

- **Alternatives**: Share recipes for natural pest deterrents that can be made from household ingredients.
- **Advocacy**: Work with local governments and organizations to limit pesticide use in public spaces.

Development of Green Corridors

Green corridors are strips of vegetation that connect isolated green spaces, allowing pollinators to move safely across urban areas. These corridors are vital for the survival of bee populations in cities, providing them with the habitats and resources needed to thrive. Urban beekeepers can champion the creation of green corridors by collaborating with city planners, landscape architects, and environmental organizations.

Actions to support the development of green corridors include:

- **Mapping**: Identify potential routes that connect existing green spaces, such as parks, gardens, and natural areas.
- **Collaboration**: Work with local authorities and community groups to design and implement green corridor projects.
- **Public Engagement**: Raise awareness about the importance of green corridors for biodiversity and encourage community participation in planting and maintenance efforts.

Promoting urban biodiversity through these strategies means urban beekeepers not only support the health and prosperity of bee populations but also contribute to the creation of more resilient and sustainable urban environments. These efforts help ensure that cities can be vibrant havens for wildlife and humans alike, fostering a harmonious coexistence that enriches our urban landscapes.

Sustainability in Hive Management

As urban beekeepers, our practices are not only measured by the health and productivity of our hives but also by the impact we have on the environment. Adopting sustainable hive management practices ensures that we contribute positively to our urban ecosystems, supporting not just our bees but the broader environment. Here, we delve into the best practices for maintaining hives sustainably, focusing on natural pest control methods, sustainable harvesting practices, and the use of eco-friendly materials in hive construction.

Natural Pest Control Methods

- **Integrated Pest Management**: IPM is a holistic approach that combines different management strategies to control pest populations while minimizing the use of chemicals. For urban beekeepers, this could mean introducing natural predators of common pests, using mechanical barriers to prevent pest access, or employing behavioral controls like hive rotation to disrupt pest life cycles.
- **Essential Oils and Organic Treatments**: Many essential oils, such as thyme oil, lemongrass oil, and eucalyptus oil, have been shown to deter pests without harming bees. These can be used in small quantities around the hive or in hive treatments. Organic acids like oxalic acid and formic acid can also be effective against varroa mites when used correctly and responsibly.
- **Cultural Practices**: Simple cultural practices, such as maintaining cleanliness around the hive, ensuring proper ventilation, and avoiding the overuse of synthetic materials, can naturally reduce pest pressures. Regular inspections and early detection of issues are also key components of a sustainable pest management strategy.

Sustainable Harvesting Practices

- **Mindful Honey Extraction**: Sustainable harvesting involves taking only surplus honey, leaving enough stores to sustain the colony through lean periods. This approach respects the bees' hard work and ensures their health and well-being. It's essential to monitor honey stores regularly and understand the natural foraging cycles in your urban environment.

- **Comb Rotation and Wax Reuse**: Regularly rotating old combs out of the hive and allowing bees to build new ones helps prevent disease buildup and encourages healthy colony growth. Old wax can be melted down and purified for use in candles, cosmetics, or even as a foundation for new combs, minimizing waste and promoting a cycle of reuse.
- **Supporting Local Forage**: Encouraging local flora that provides forage for bees year-round supports not only your hives but the broader ecosystem. Planting bee-friendly flowers, shrubs, and trees, and engaging with community initiatives to create green spaces, are practices that ensure the sustainability of urban beekeeping.

Eco-friendly Materials in Hive Construction

- **Sustainable Sourcing**: Choosing materials for hive construction and maintenance that are renewable, sustainably harvested, or recycled can significantly reduce the environmental footprint of beekeeping. Wood from certified sustainable forests, recycled plastic for hive components, and natural finishes like linseed oil are all eco-conscious choices.
- **Longevity and Durability**: Investing in high-quality materials that withstand the elements and the test of time not only is more sustainable but also ensures the health and safety of the bee colony. Durable materials reduce the need for frequent replacements, lowering the overall environmental impact.
- **Biodegradable and Non-toxic Materials**: Whenever possible, using biodegradable materials for hive components that come into direct contact with bees, such as hive frames or foundation, ensures that if they degrade or need to be disposed of, they won't harm the environment. Similarly, non-toxic paints and finishes should be used externally to protect both bees and the environment.

Incorporating these sustainable practices into hive management not only benefits the bee colonies we care for but also contributes to the health and resilience of our urban environments. By adopting a mindful approach to beekeeping, we can ensure that our activities support the well-being of our cities, our communities, and the planet.

Educating the Next Generation

The sustainability of urban beekeeping and the broader goals of environmental stewardship hinge significantly on the education of the next generation. By instilling a sense of responsibility and curiosity about the natural world in young minds, we lay the foundation for a future that values and actively contributes to the preservation of biodiversity within our urban landscapes. This section delves into the various initiatives aimed at incorporating beekeeping and environmental stewardship into educational curriculums, youth programs, and community workshops, highlighting the pivotal role these endeavors play in securing the future of urban beekeeping.

Integrating Beekeeping into Educational Curriculums

Schools have a unique opportunity to introduce students to the wonders and complexities of beekeeping, embedding it within the fabric of their environmental science or biology curriculums. Through hands-on learning experiences, students can gain insights into the life cycle of bees, the importance of pollinators in our ecosystem, and the basics of hive management. Such initiatives not only enrich the educational experience but also foster a sense of environmental responsibility from a young age.

- **Case Studies and Project-Based Learning**: Incorporating case studies of urban beekeeping projects into lessons can provide real-world context to theoretical knowledge, while project-based learning initiatives can encourage students to engage directly with beekeeping practices, under guided supervision.
- **School Beekeeping Clubs**: Establishing beekeeping clubs as extracurricular activities provides interested students with the opportunity to dive deeper into the subject, offering more hands-on experiences with hive management and honey harvesting.

Youth Programs and Community Engagement

Beyond the classroom, youth programs and community workshops serve as vital platforms for spreading awareness and knowledge about urban beekeeping and environmental stewardship. These programs can be tailored to engage children and teenagers, creating interactive and educational experiences that highlight the significance of bees to our urban ecosystems.

- **Beekeeping Workshops for Youth**: Specialized workshops designed for younger audiences can demystify the process of beekeeping, presenting it in an accessible and engaging manner. These workshops can cover topics from the basics of bee biology to the environmental impact of bees, and even practical sessions on bee-friendly gardening.
- **Community Pollinator Projects**: Engaging young people in community pollinator projects, such as creating bee gardens or installing solitary bee hotels, can provide hands-on experiences that reinforce the importance of pollinators. These projects also offer the added benefit of beautifying community spaces and fostering a sense of collective responsibility towards our environment.

Building Partnerships for Educational Outreach

The success of educational initiatives often relies on the strength of partnerships between schools, beekeeping associations, environmental organizations, and local governments. These partnerships can provide the resources, expertise, and support necessary to develop comprehensive educational programs that reach a broad audience.

- **Collaborative Curriculum Development**: Working together, educators and beekeeping experts can develop curriculum materials that accurately reflect the challenges and opportunities of urban beekeeping, ensuring that educational content is both engaging and informative.

- **Community Support and Resources**: Leveraging community support can provide the resources needed to sustain educational programs, from funding for beekeeping equipment to access to local green spaces for practical learning experiences.

In summary, educating the next generation about urban beekeeping and environmental stewardship is essential for the sustainability of bee populations and the broader goal of creating resilient urban ecosystems. Through school curriculums, youth programs, and community workshops, we can inspire a new generation of environmental advocates, equipped with the knowledge and skills to continue the important work of urban beekeeping and to champion the health of our planet.

©Anthony Carter | www.beekeeping-101.com |part of Carman Online Content Publishing Ltd

Book Conclusion

As we draw the final pages of "Urban Beekeeping: Managing Hives in City Environments" to a close, we extend our deepest gratitude to you, the reader, for embarking on this enlightening journey with us. Your interest and dedication to understanding the nuances of urban beekeeping not only reflects a commitment to the well-being of bees, but also signals a broader concern for our urban ecosystems and the world we share. Beekeeping in the cityscape is more than a hobby; it is a powerful act of environmental stewardship, a bridge connecting us to nature amidst the concrete and steel of our urban environments, and a testament to the resilience and adaptability of both bees and humans.

This book was conceived as a guide, a companion to assist you through the complexities and rewards of urban beekeeping. We hope that the knowledge shared within these pages inspires you to pursue your beekeeping journey, whether you're taking your first steps or looking to deepen your existing practice. The path of an urban beekeeper is filled with challenges, learning opportunities, and the undeniable joy of contributing to the sustainability of our cities and the health of our planet.

As you close this book, remember that the journey does not end here. The future of urban beekeeping, and indeed the future of our urban landscapes, is in the hands of informed, passionate individuals like you. We encourage you to continue learning, exploring, and sharing your experiences with the community. Together, we can ensure that the buzz of bees remains a vital part of our urban tapestry for generations to come.

Thank you for reading, for caring, and for acting. May your hives thrive, your gardens blossom, and your urban beekeeping adventures contribute to a greener, more connected world.

©Anthony Carter | www.beekeeping-101.com | part of Carman Online Content Publishing Ltd

Thank You

Thank you for joining me on this exploration of urban beekeeping. If this book has enriched your understanding, inspired your practice, or contributed to your urban beekeeping journey in any way, I would love to hear from you.

Please consider leaving a review on the platform where you purchased this book. Your feedback is invaluable—not only does it help me to improve and grow, but it also aids fellow bee enthusiasts in discovering the joys and challenges of urban beekeeping.

Share your thoughts, experiences, and how this book has impacted your beekeeping adventure. Together, we can spread the buzz and support thriving bee communities in our cities. Thank you for your support and for being an essential part of this journey. It is so very much appreciated.

©Anthony Carter | www.beekeeping-101.com |part of Carman Online Content Publishing Ltd